THABANI ZULU
CA (SA)

Risk and Reward

Start and run a successful small business in South Africa

TAFELBERG

Tafelberg
An imprint of NB Publishers
40 Heerengracht, Cape Town, 8000
www.tafelberg.com
© 2010 Thabani Zulu

All rights reserved
No part of this book may be reproduced or transmitted in any form or by any electronic or mechanical means, including photocopying and recording, or by any other information storage or retrieval system, without written permission from the publisher

Set in Minion
Edited by Linde Dietrich
Cover design by Michele Staples
Book design by Nazli Jacobs

Printed and bound by Ultra Litho, South Africa
First edition, first impression 2010

ISBN: 978-0-624-04888-6

Contents

PREFACE 11

1. A PURPOSE BIGGER THAN YOU 13
   - The dangers of a quest for immediate gratification 14
   - Dining with crowned heads 16
   - Bringing God into your business 16

2. BUSINESS AND RISKS 18
   - The difference between a risk and a crisis 22
   - Risk management 22
   - A quick look at the business risks 24
   - Business risks in detail 26
   - Managing the risks 28
   - The risk of not managing risks 30

3. DECIDING ON YOUR BUSINESS 31
   - Your personal aspirations 32
   - Competition 37
   - Barriers to entry 40
   - Touching base with those in business 42
   - Am I fit for business? 43

4. BUILDING A BUSINESS MODEL 46
   - A model of your business 46
   - Your product/service 48
   - Your market/customers 49
   - Your competition 52
   - The environment 55
   - Your management 56

5. CHOOSING YOUR PARTNERS 58
   - Can you make it on your own? 58
   - Can you afford not to have a partner? 59
   - Partnership versus employment 60
   - Choosing a partner 60
   - Forms of ownership 62
   - A sole proprietorship 63
   - A partnership 64
   - A close corporation(CC) 66
   - A company 67

6. FINANCING YOUR BUSINESS 70
   - Equity financing 71
   - Debt financing 72
   - What are the considerations with debt finance? 73
   - The financing institutions 77
   - What types of finance are available? 78
   - Some tips about financing your business 81

7. BUYING AN EXISTING BUSINESS 83
   - Does buying an existing business make sense? 83
   - What must you know before you buy? 85
   - The financial statements 87
   - Attaching a value to the business 90
   - Book value 93
   - Multiple earnings 94
   - Discounted cash flows 95
   - A few words of advice 97

8. DRAWING UP A BUSINESS PLAN 98
   - What is a business plan? 98
   - Uses of a business plan 100
   - Putting a business plan together 100
   - Basic elements of a business plan 101

- Detail of the business plan 103
- A final word on the business plan 112

9. DRAWING UP A BUDGET 113
    - What is a budget? 113
    - What if there is no budget? 114
    - How do you put a budget together? 115
    - Management of the budget 126

10. PRODUCT COSTING 128
    - Cost accumulation 129
    - Cost allocation to product 132
    - Setting a price for your product 133
    - Price and competition 135
    - Pricing for two or more products 136
    - Manufacturing businesses 139
    - Service businesses 140
    - Problems with costing 141

11. MARKETING YOUR BUSINESS 142
    - Attracting customers 143
    - Retaining your customer base 145
    - Marketing 149
    - Segmentation analysis 155
    - Customer service 157

12. EMPLOYING PEOPLE 159
    - South African employment legislation 160
    - Appointment 161
    - Benefits and deductions 163
    - Engaging employees 166
    - Retention 168
    - Termination 169
    - Contract workers 171

13. FINANCIAL ADMINISTRATION 172
   - What is financial administration? 172
   - Transactions 173
   - Flow of transactions through the accounting system 174
   - Accounting packages 182

14. MANAGING SUPPLIERS 183
   - Assessing your suppliers 184
   - Developing a comprehensive supply strategy 185
   - Negotiating with suppliers 188

15. MANAGING TAXES 192
   - Why taxation? 192
   - The South African tax system 193
   - Income tax 194
   - Deductions and allowances 197
   - Value-added tax 199
   - Turnover tax 205
   - Employees' tax 205
   - Skills development levy 207

A FINAL WORD 209

APPENDIX: REPAYMENT CALCULATOR 210

INDEX 213

ABOUT THE AUTHOR 217

The dynamics surrounding your business

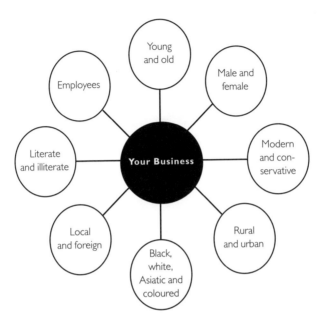

Preface

This book is designed to be a step-by-step guide to starting, managing and even selling your business. By focusing on the risks you will encounter and proposing strategies for managing them, it aims to answer many of the questions you might be faced with in your quest to be a successful business person. I would love this book to be in the office of everyone who runs a business and to be used as a reference guide when you are confronted with difficult decisions.

This guide is obviously not comprehensive. You will appreciate that the dynamics of a business are vast, ranging from business finance and marketing to managing contracts, suppliers, clients and human resources. All these fields are disciplines in their own right and cannot be covered in depth in a publication such as this. For your benefit I have, however, attempted to condense the material and provide introductions to critical concepts. This should enable you to make the decisions you intend making, but will not make you a specialist in the fields concerned. I would advise that, when in doubt as you venture and grow your business, you contact specialists in the various fields for more guidance and support.

I have kept the material as practical as possible, shying away from theory that may be irrelevant to you. The illustrations and examples in this book are real. They reflect the experiences of many of the business people I have interacted with. Some of them, good or bad, will happen to you too! Take them seriously, and learn to anticipate and deal with such challenges.

The book is relevant to South African business, big or small. While the principles it covers can be applied universally, I have used South African legislation, culture and business language to make it as applicable as possible to a South African business person.

I trust you will find the material beneficial and useful in your endeavour to run a successful business. I wish you well; the road will be steep and hard, but the reward that lies ahead is the fruit of your labour. Hang in there, and do not despair. Be wise, be fast, and be purposeful!

Good luck!

Thabani Zulu
March 2010

CHAPTER 1

A purpose bigger than you

- What is the purpose of my business?
- How do we define success?
- Do I have to choose between integrity and business success?
- What do I want for the future of my business?

I would have liked to get straight into the essence of my book, discussing how you can manage the risks in business and impressing on you the various strategies of getting your business to fly, but I thought, no. In South Africa today there is so much more to keep in mind when you think about the business landscape. There is so much at risk. As a matter of fact, the biggest risk to the success of your business today is *you*!

Business has become notorious worldwide, known for greed and selfishness and polluted by quick-win, unsustainable transactions. Business has become a lions' den, possessed by materialism and wealth accumulation as opposed to the pursuit of sustainable growth and prosperity.

There is much more than purely business-related questions that you need to consider as you run your business. What are you doing this for? Is it to create a legacy of empowering others, or is it solely for your own material gain? Do you want your business to live on after your death, or do you not mind if it dies with you? Are you in it for your own recognition, or for the recognition of your business? Is your purpose a narrow one of self-interest and short-term gain, or is it one that is bigger than you and takes the good of society into account? The answers to these questions can determine the success or the failure of your business.

The dangers of a quest for immediate gratification

The biggest enemy of business is the desire to grow too big, too quickly. Many aspiring entrepreneurs feel this urge immediately when they get into business. It is as if they think society will judge them as failures if they do not have the latest vehicle, carry the fanciest cellphone and live in a palatial home. They lose what I term "the essence of business", which is putting the business before yourself. You see this behaviour as soon as the funds come through from the financier, or when the business makes a profit, or when there is cash in the business's bank account. The mind goes wild; the business itself is forgotten, "the dream deferred".

With this quest for immediate gratification come a number of evils. Evils that can easily be avoided by being patient and understanding that the road to success and financial freedom is a long and tedious one. Evils that eventually catch up with the entrepreneur and result in exactly what he or she was attempting to avoid: poverty, humiliation and shame.

Compromised decisions

The business world is riddled with fraud and corruption. I worked for government in forensic investigations for years, and what I realised is that as much as people in public office are to be blamed for this, they do not act alone! Behind them are wealthy business people who are constantly enticing them with kickbacks in return for contracts. This has become such a plague that every entrepreneur wants to find an insider who will throw contracts at them in exchange for something. Resist the temptation of being lured into quick contracts in exchange for bribes. While the reality is that you may not get certain contracts in this current climate if you do not go along with this trend, refuse to compromise yourself and your business. If values such as integrity, honesty and hard work are the foundation of your business, you will succeed in the long run.

Definition of success

We live in a world that defines success in material terms. The bigger the car you drive, the more successful you are! This has reshaped the way we do business, hence the quest for immediate gratification. The moment you define your success away from this generally accepted definition will be the day you start to succeed in business. I am not discouraging people from accumulating wealth, but I am suggesting that you should have a much broader definition of success that includes the good of society as well: one that recognises the empowerment of others, social responsibility, and satisfying the future needs of those who will survive you.

Let me try to explain what I believe to be the pillars of success:

1. **Financial freedom.** I might as well start with this even though I do not consider it the primary pillar of success. You want to be able to sustain yourself, and in these times when money rules the world, you want to be able to afford the basic needs (your health, security, food on the table) and spoil yourself with the things you yearn for. We live on this earth only once, and we want to make the best of it.
2. **Social acceptance.** I do not believe you are successful if the world around you does not accept you; if people do not trust you, if you add no value in people's lives, and if society cannot rely on you. You may be a millionaire, but if society knows that your wealth is the result of "blood money" or corruption, you cannot be proud of it – even though you may put up a bold front and brag about it. The truth is, if society curses you for it, if your conscience is uncomfortable with it, you will not enjoy it. It is not success!
3. **Intellectual strength.** Let's face it – you do not merely want to be "lucky": to find yourself in the right place at the right time and stumble upon a million by chance. You do not want to know that had you not been "connected", you would not be where you are. I am not downplaying the importance of luck or connections, but knowing that your brains made it happen gives you gratification. Knowing that you stretched your intellectual muscles to achieve your wealth makes you feel good about yourself. While I am not suggesting that a formal edu-

cation is essential, I would advise it, particularly for the youth. Just to be known as intellectually and technically sound in your field creates a feeling of success.
4. **Social responsibility.** This must not be confused with social acceptance, as social responsibility refers to compassion and sharing. If life has put you in a position of prosperity, success means not staying there alone. Lift others with you. It need not be money and donations, but could be any means by which you help to create a future for others. Do give your skills or dedicate your time for the benefit of another human being.
5. **Sustainability.** Success is also the creation of a legacy. You should realise that you are mortal and that future generations should enjoy the benefit of your hard work. Your family should be able to survive after your death, and your employees should not have to lose their jobs when you pass away. Your name must live on!

Dining with crowned heads

Business is about relationships, granted, but in South Africa this is a bit overdone. Often people are discouraged from going into business because they do not know anyone in high positions or are not associated with prominent politicians. Those in business sometimes spend enormous amounts of time trying to cultivate these relationships instead of devoting the same attention to their businesses. I am not undermining the value of having "connectivity" in business, in fact, I discuss this aspect in one of the chapters in this book. But a winning concept with a winning product requires less of such connectivity. Focus more on your business.

Bringing God into your business

You need the presence of God in your business. You need His blessings. You need Him in every decision you take, every move you make. Here are some pointers on how you can bring Him into your venture:

1. Let your business concept be holy. You cannot hope to succeed if your success depends on the failure of others. Your concept must be beneficial to your customers, must not disadvantage your suppliers, must not exploit your labour, and must not harm the environment.
2. Let your decisions be holy. You will be faced with tough decisions in business. Decide in a manner that pleases God. Do not take the path that will lead you to instant gratification at the expense of your conscience.
3. Let your money be holy. Do not run a business in which you have to look over your shoulder. Stay sure that your conscience is clean, and you will not be putting out fires, bribing investigators and running away from the law. Declare your income for tax purposes. You may not have money to pay, but do not run away. Acknowledge your debts, face those to whom you owe money.
4. Let your relationships be holy. Avoid mixing with those who want to use you in unscrupulous deals for their benefit and at the expense of your business. Let it stay strong! Resist diabolical delights and get closer to God every day. You will face pressure, but manoeuvre through it in ways that will leave your soul unharmed.
5. Let your actions be holy. You have been privileged to be in business. Maybe it is God's way of providing for others through you. Do not disappoint Him. Give! And give unreservedly. As long as you look after His children, He will look after you.

CHAPTER 2

Business and risks

> - What risks am I faced with in business?
> - How do I manage the risks?
> - What can cause my business to fail?
> - How can I avoid failure?

The old adage that business is taking risks for a reward is very true. If you want a safe income stream, rather go for employment in a stable company. You know that at the end of the month you will receive your income. All the risks, including the risk that you might not get paid, are borne by the owners of the company and they should ensure that you receive what is due to you come month-end.

The minute you want to go into business, however, you must accept that you are taking a number of very serious risks in order to earn a reward. Hopefully, that reward is higher than the salary you would otherwise be earning; if this is not the case, there was really no point in venturing into business. Your life must then be a series of processes and strategies to manage the risks you face. Failure to manage these risks can lead to the failure of your business. How many people have you come across who were unsuccessful in business because:

1. they were hit badly by overheads;
2. they had a series of break-ins and thefts;

3. their staff stole from them;
4. their supplier was liquidated and they could not find alternative suppliers; or
5. they were themselves liquidated by the banks because they were unable to repay their loans?

In this book I hope to impress on you that once you get into business, your life must be spent managing risks such as these. I hope to convey the message that although the risks exist, they can be minimised and managed. I do not claim that my management strategies are the best out there, or that my suggestions are exhaustive. Business is dynamic, and there are many factors at play. You will be in a particular situation that demands that you think outside the box and come up with creative ideas to manage the specific risks you are confronted with. I will simply highlight risks and propose management strategies. You will evaluate these strategies and implement them if they suit your specific circumstances.

In the following chapters, we will discuss the dynamics of business. You will realise that in every aspect of your business there will be risks: financial risks, operational risks, legal risks and strategic risks. Doing nothing about them and wishing them away could result in the collapse of your business, which I am sure you do not want.

I spent some time doing research in the course of the development of this book, and what I found was even worse than I had anticipated. Did you know that 85% of new businesses fail in the first five years of their operation? In fact, only one new company in ten survives beyond ten years. I do not know what you think, but I find it alarming. It means that the probability of failure within five years is 85%! Experts blame this high failure rate on poor risk management, poor tactics to get the business known and accepted in the market, and poor financial management.

I went to the internet and found hundreds of companies that have experienced failure, bankruptcy and liquidation. Some of them were highly reputable companies: Automobili Lamborghini in 1978, Daewoo in 1999, Planet Hollywood in 1999 and in 2001, Arthur Andersen in 2002, Parmalat in 2003, and many others. The major problems were in the areas of sales and finances. Let us just look briefly at a few companies that have seen these risks materialising[1]:

Harold's Stores, Inc.

Founded in 1948, Harold's was a Dallas-based chain of stores that sold traditional, high-end, classic-styled ladies' and men's clothing. The chain operated 43 stores in 19 mid-western and south-eastern states in the United States, usually located in upper-class areas and shopping centres. Prior to its bankruptcy filing, the company employed 624 people.

When the company was granted bankruptcy liquidation on 10 November 2008, it claimed that "increased competition and a weak economy have left us no choice but to cease operations".

Oasis Hong Kong Airlines Limited

This is a now defunct long-haul, low-cost airline that was based in Hong Kong. It operated scheduled services to London's Gatwick Airport and Vancouver International Airport from its hub, Hong Kong International Airport.

Oasis was one of a growing number of long-haul passenger airlines that adopted a budget airline model pioneered by the now defunct Laker Airways Skytrain service in the 1970s. Oasis was voted "World's Leading New Airline" at the Annual World Travel Awards 2007.

Much of the original success of Oasis Hong Kong was due to the airline's widely advertised minimum fares. However, fares later became much less competitive.

On 9 April 2008, Oasis Hong Kong announced that it had ceased operations, and a provisional liquidator, KPMG China, had been appointed to oversee the liquidation of the company. On 8 July 2008 it was announced that unsecured creditors of the collapsed company,

---

1 The information in this section was obtained from *Wikipedia, the free encyclopedia*.

including ticket holders, would eventually receive no more than 10% of what they were owed, according to KPMG.

Nationwide Airlines

Most readers probably remember the well-publicised story of this South African company's problems and eventual collapse. Before halting its operations in 2008, Nationwide Airlines operated scheduled domestic and international services from its main base at OR Tambo International Airport, Johannesburg. It was privately owned and had 800 employees (at March 2007).

Founded in 1995 by Chief Executive Vernon Bricknell, the airline began operating charter services within Africa for the United Nations and the World Food Programme, as well as ad hoc passenger and cargo charters. Nationwide Airlines was one of four companies within the group, along with Nationwide Air Charter, Nationwide Aircraft Maintenance and Nationwide Aircraft Support, and started domestic scheduled operations in December 1995. In 2003, Nationwide inaugurated an intercontinental service with wide-body aircraft. In February 2005, the airline began updating its fleet by introducing its first Boeing 737-500, becoming the only operator of the -500 type in South Africa.

In March 2008, Nationwide was recognised as the most punctual scheduled airline in 2007 between London and Johannesburg for the second consecutive year, according to UK Civil Aviation Authority statistics.

In 2007, the airline experienced a number of problems and was grounded for a while for non-compliance with South African Civil Aviation regulations. In January 2008 Nationwide resumed operations and attained a gradual recovery of the business. However, in the months of March and April they were faced with a 30% increase in fuel costs coupled with a decrease in passenger loads. Nationwide's cash flow became critical, and as a result, the airline decided to voluntarily cease all flight operations until further notice. Operations were halted on 29 April 2008.

I hope you can identify, just from these few examples, some of the risks you will be faced with in business. Most of them may not cause your business to collapse, as was the case with these big companies, but they may result in significant losses of revenue and profits, loss of market share which will take you a long time to recover from, and loss of reputation. These risks must be managed.

The difference between a risk and a crisis

One thing to remember from the outset is that a risk is not a crisis. By the time you are faced with a crisis, it is often too late. Your mind is already in reactive mode, and you are already putting out a fire – a risk has materialised. *A risk is a potential crisis which has not yet materialised, and which, if not managed adequately, can result in a crisis.* The crisis is in the future.

This distinction already makes life a lot easier. When you deal with a risk, your mind is proactive. Your senses, though strained by fear, are calmed by the fact that it has not happened, and your attention is less sidetracked than when you are running an operation to put out a fire. You are more sober and clear-headed.

My advice is, do not allow yourself to be in a position where you are reactive in managing unwanted situations in your business. Try to anticipate danger, deal with it proactively, and avoid being hit unawares. Finding yourself in such a situation can be very stressful and, as I have mentioned, it may be too late!

Risk management

You probably know it already – risk management is the art of managing risks, the technique of a leader in anticipating danger and putting systems in place to protect the business from such danger before it happens.

Anticipation

It begins with anticipation.

Can you imagine what a world of difference it would have made to the lives of the companies that I referred to above if they could have anticipated the dangers that hit them, and reacted accordingly? Of course, I speak with the benefit of hindsight and as an external observer. The truth is, they were in the hot seat, faced with doom and racing against the inevitable. The risk had materialised! The first question is, how well did they anticipate this?

The more you can anticipate, the better you can manage. You do not want to say, "I did not see it coming!" You want to see almost everything coming, or planning to come. This capacity is critical. You can acquire it by reading up on as many businesses as you can, especially those that have collapsed. Find out why, because you really do not want to fall into the same trap. Engage professionals in the field and ask them to help you anticipate potential risks. Be very negative; after all, that is the nature of risk. Instead of being over-optimistic, ask yourself, "What can go wrong in my business?"

Management

The next step is to develop a strategy and processes to deal with the identified risks. Your strategy should be underpinned by three questions:

1. How can I *prevent* it from happening?
2. How can I *detect* that it has happened?
3. How can I quickly put out the fire and *correct* the damage when it happens?

Trust me, business owners who are defrauded or stolen from internally by their employees do not see it until it is too late because question 2 was never answered in their risk management strategy. Those who get their cars stolen and lose business did not answer question 3. Those who experience one crisis after another suffer because they neglected to answer question 1.

For almost every major or significant risk that your business faces, you must answer the questions above. You truly cannot get past the risk without satisfying yourself that the answers make sense.

A quick look at the business risks

If you reflect on it for a moment, your business is a risk from the day you start it to the day you get out of it one way or the other. In this book I will be discussing the risks and strategies to manage them in successive chapters, and covering the topics below:

- **Product**
  What if I go into business with the wrong product?
  What if my product does not sell?
  What if there is no sustainable market for my product?
- **Partnering**
  What if I get the wrong partners?
  What if the structure of my business is wrong?
- **Finance**
  What if I cannot raise capital for my business?
  What if the finance I get is too expensive for the business?
  What if I do not make a profit?
  What if my costs go up?
- **Competition**
  What if my business is wiped out by competitors?
  What if the market prefers to buy from the competition?
- **Employees**
  What if I employ the wrong people for my business?
  What if the employees go on strike?
  What if the employees become redundant and costly?
- **Suppliers**
  What if the suppliers go out of business?
  What if the suppliers take long to deliver?

What if the suppliers are expensive?
What if the suppliers deliver poor quality?
- **Taxes**
What if I get on the wrong side of the law?
What if I fail to pay or declare my taxes?

The following diagram gives an indication of the risks to which a typical business is exposed in its life cycle:

INCEPTION →	OPERATION →	DISPOSAL
Sector	Cash flow	Valuation
Valuation	Losses	Economy
Finance	Transport	Buyer availability
Security	Suppliers	
Competition	Market	
	Human resources	
	Environment	
	Taxes	
	Legal	

I think we need to ponder on each one of these risks. You will see from the above diagram that there are just so many factors that can cause a business to collapse. Many are still missing, I am sure, but I have tried to capture those risks I would consider significant. Each risk may be so significant that it exerts strain on the business throughout its life. For instance, if you enter into an inappropriate finance contract, it can cause stressed cash flows and sustained losses, and, even on disposal, affect the valuation of the business so negatively that the buyers pick it up for next to nothing.

I had a business that was badly financed and structured. Every day was a battle, and every cent that I made seemed to be swallowed up by finance costs. The infrastructure was bigger than the operation. There was no way of getting out because of the unfavourable contracts I had entered into. Cash flows were severely strained and the business was eventually liquidated by the financiers, where it was sold under the hammer for a pittance.

As I write this book, I am still recovering from the aftermath of my bad risk management! You would be wise to learn from the voice of experience and not let it happen to you.

Business risks in detail

I want us to look into these risks in greater detail. I am hoping that you will be able to identify where your business is and therefore which risks you should be managing.

INCEPTION	RISK
Sector	• The sector is not vibrant and sustainably profitable • The sector is heavily legislated • The business is not duly registered
Valuation	• The business is overvalued • The underlying value is not substantiated and cannot be realised • You have inadequate capacity to unlock the value you will pay for
Finance	• You do not have finance for the venture • You may overcapitalise your business • A financial institution studies your business plan and declines • The business plan is of an inferior standard
Security	• You do not have security for the finance • Offering security exposes you and your family to more risks
Competition	• Competitors are fierce and unforgiving • There is just too much competition • You do not have a competitive edge

OPERATION

Cash flow	• Not enough cash to discharge obligations • Not enough cash to buy needed material • Bad credit rating due to non-payment
Losses	• Break-ins • Shrinkages
Transport	• Inadequate • Not in a working condition • High maintenance costs
Suppliers	• Insufficient, with heavy reliance on a few • Expensive • Delivery lead times not adequate • Deliver poor quality
Market	• Too small • Very fussy and makes many returns • Unfavourable economic conditions, therefore poor payment • Delays in payment affecting cash flows • Aggressive and more tactical opposition
Human resources	• Non-availability of necessary skills • Labour unrest • Loss of necessary workforce • Lack of productivity
Environment	• Product potentially harmful to the environment • Environmental impact assessments not conducted on time
Taxes	• Late payments attracting interest and penalties • Inadequate skills regarding tax issues and filing of returns
Legal	• Non-compliance with legislation • Litigation by suppliers, employees and clients

DISPOSAL

Valuation	• Value of the business is too low
	• Cannot find a business valuer at an affordable price
Economy	• Value is too low due to prevailing economic climate
	• Non-affordability due to economic climate
Buyer availability	• Non-availability of serious buyers who can afford the price
	• Inadequate purchase and sale contract

Managing the risks

Since you now know what risks your business faces, you are in a much better position to manage them. Remember that the process of identifying risks is an ongoing one and that the dynamics of your business will keep changing from time to time, exposing you to new risks. Do not regard this as a static process that unfolds only once in the life of your business, otherwise you will miss potential risks.

I will not deal with each risk here, because the strategies to manage them will vary from business to business and from person to person. Some of us are dangerous risk takers and will forge ahead despite the risk exposure. Although the accountant in me discourages that, I am reminded of what one of my friends said to me on this issue: "If you want to succeed in business, get rid of your accountant or risk manager. He will scare you sufficiently for you to want to do nothing eventually!" So take what I am saying with a pinch of salt, but please, at least know what risks you are up against before you take a decision on how to deal with them.

Prevention

Treatment, as I indicated earlier, can be preventive. As the doctors say, "Prevention is better than cure", and the same principle applies in business. You want to put systems in place to ensure that the risk is prevented, because you will spend twice as much energy and resources to cure the problem if it materialises. Install burglar gates and alarms in your warehouse.

Fit the company vehicles with immobilisers. Draw up Human Resources policies to instruct your employees on how you want things to be done. Invest in accounting and costing packages to ensure that the product costs are accurate and you do not sell at a loss. In other words, prevent the risks from happening.

Detection

Prevention systems are not a foolproof guarantee that risks will not occur, so you want to go to the next level of risk management – detection. You want to have systems in place to inform you that you have been hit. There is no point in going on with business as usual when things are seriously wrong in the heart of your business. You are losing food stock every day because your employees are stealing it. Your vehicles are travelling everywhere, costing you petrol and maintenance, but not bringing in any money. You want to be able to detect these things early enough, so your systems must allow for that. The stock must be counted frequently. The logbooks for the vehicles must be filled in, signed and checked. You or your senior people or yourself must contact the clients regularly to check whether they are happy with your service. Mechanisms to inform you that something is wrong must be put in place and applied diligently.

Correction

Believe it or not, both prevention and detection mechanisms may not be enough to ensure that the risk is being effectively managed. Sometimes they may be so costly that you want to minimise them and place more emphasis on corrective mechanisms. For example, the fact that I have an anti-hijack device, an immobiliser and a tracker in my car does not offer absolute protection against its being stolen or a guarantee that it will be recovered. The risk is still there – it may have been minimised, but it is still there. You may just want to go for a corrective control mechanism, one that suggests that you have been hit and places you in the same situation you were in before the risk occurred. In this case, just get insurance. You may also take out legal cover for potential litigation by suppliers and customers, and so on.

The risk of not managing risks

I want to drum this point home as much as I can. *Not managing risks is risky in itself.* It is negligent and not businesslike. You are exposing your business to unwanted, unpleasant surprises.

You are putting yourself and your employees in a fire-fighting mode and, believe me, you will be putting out fires for the rest of your life until you get this right.

The rest of this book is premised on effective risk management. In the chapters that follow, I propose solutions for managing fundamental risks that may cause your business not to grow as fast as you want or, at worst, to collapse. We will discuss issues of finance, employment, administration, competition and many others. All have risks associated with them that you need to manage. I would like you to follow me through this material and try to correct the mistakes before you make them. This will make your business thrive!

CHAPTER 3

Deciding on your business

- Am I made for this?
- Do I have the time?
- What business must I start?
- Does this business have a market?
- What about the competition?
- Will I make money doing this?

Setting up a business is not easy. It requires a lot of planning, financial resources and emotional investment. By the time you realise that you have entered into a wrong venture, it may be too late. Therefore, it is critical that you make the right choice when deciding on a business venture. Be careful not to be "a Jack of all trades", and venture into everything at the risk of not being seen as a specialist, and failing to attract a specific market. There is a dangerous surge in South Africa of companies being registered that purport to be able to do everything, such as ABC Enterprise CC selling stationery, road construction, building, catering services, facilitation and training. The old adage "Jack of all trades, master of none" still holds true. There are many ventures that you can enter into, for example:

1. property development;
2. catering;
3. maize production;
4. security; or
5. business consulting.

In this chapter, I want us to explore some of the critical factors that you should take into consideration before deciding which business to enter into.

Your personal aspirations

In this discussion, it is important to realise upfront that you may not be alone in the business you intend starting. We will look at this issue in more detail in Chapter 5: Choosing your partners. But whether you are alone or in a group, the sum total of "you" must possess the attributes that we will discuss in this section.

Most businesses fail because of the owner or owners. They set it up because they believed it would be profitable, and ignored the fact that they would have to run it to profitability. Perhaps it is not in line with their interests, they lack the time and energy to manage it, and they generally find it "boring" to run. Running your own business takes up more time than being employed, therefore you need to ask yourself if you have the time. If you don't, do not bother getting into business, because it simply will not work. It will take *you* to make your business survive and succeed.

One of my acquaintances decided to take the leap and resign from work to start a business. What transpired later were his fundamental reasons for taking such a step. He was angry with his employer and thought he was underpaid and not being promoted to a position of power. His motivations were power and greed. He did not have the energy, in fact he was simply too lazy to run a business, even though he wanted to own one. All he prided himself on was that he had a business of his own and could produce proof of this in the form of business cards and company profiles. That gave him the glory, but it was short-lived.

Area of interest

Choose an area that you have a passion for and enjoy engaging in. Do not get into agriculture if you find it too dirty and hope you will employ a manager to run the business for you. Your hands must get dirty. After all, it is your business!

Have you noticed how successful you become in areas that really interest you? As a schoolboy I used to know a song by heart from the day it was released, yet never managed to memorise significant history dates and events. My history marks were abysmal, but my musical knowledge was superb! That was my area of interest, and it became my area of excellence. Business is not so dissimilar. You become great and successful at what you enjoy waking up in the morning to do. Your passion becomes easy to spot and will gain you the support of clients and other business associates.

Skills

Choose a business that you have the skill to manage as an individual or as a collective. We will discuss choosing partners in Chapter 5, but do not get into a business that you have no knowledge of. You will be abused by your business associates; you will not know what decisions to take in times of crisis, and you will not know how best to drive your business forward.

I recall that there was once much hype about information technology (IT) businesses and every young man wanted to get into IT. The millennium (Y2K) hurricane was blowing all around, and everyone thought they could make a killing. Hardware and software solutions were everywhere! The problem was that IT was still a highly specialised area, and people needed to know what they were getting themselves into. Many who bought hardware failed to sell it because they could not give the necessary technical demonstrations to customers. Many who were given rights by overseas companies to distribute software could not do so because they were unable to answer the basic questions that clients posed in order to take the decisions to buy such software. They did not have the skills to succeed in such businesses, even when there were opportunities.

Attitude

You attitude towards entering into business plays a vital role in determining your success or failure. If you get into business to "try it out", you will probably fail. If you get into business with the determination to succeed, however, chances are that you will. This does not mean you enter into business with no sense of the practical dynamics that we will explore throughout this book, but you enter with a winning spirit that will result in a winning business. Do not enter into business expecting quick success. It will not come, and you will despair. It will be a long and dusty road to freedom. It will have pitfalls, some so major that they make you doubt the very decision to venture into business. Some hurdles will be too high. A strong sense of perseverance and resilience will come in handy on your road to freedom. Your most likely recipe for success will be to focus your attention a lot more on the end goal whilst manoeuvring through the storms!

Business experts will tell you that it takes about 24 months for a typical business to start taking off. There are businesses that I have controlled and run for the past three years, and I am still not seeing my way clearly as far as their future is concerned. Some days I just want to shut up shop and start something else. The truth, though, is that these businesses are new, and in the midst of competition you cannot just expect the market to trust you instead of seasoned and established players. You have to penetrate slowly and make painfully tiresome strides on your road to success.

Your personality

Let's face it, running a business is about making money. Money does not fly from the sky. It comes from somebody. This means that as you make money, somebody else is losing it. The question is: do you have the nerve and personality to charge people? Yes, you may and should find this easy if you are confident of the value they get from you in exchange for their money: a quality product or a decent service. You will come across those who need your product but cannot afford it; friends who want to eat free of charge in your restaurant, or family members who feel entitled to your products or services for nothing. You will need to draw the line somewhere – the question is, can you?

My friend's restaurant business collapsed because of family members who ate at his expense whenever they were hungry. He was running a restaurant in central Durban and literally ran it dry because he was cooking for family and friends every night and every weekend. His problem was that he could not say no. He felt it would be selfish to do so and that he would lose their blessings if he drew the line. He did not run his restaurant successfully and was eventually bought out.

In business you will have to negotiate for the benefit of your business, whatever it may be. Realise that those across the table with whom you will be negotiating also have the best interests of *their* businesses at heart. You will need to be strong and sharp, but you will also need to be reasonable. You will have to be very aware of the outer limits and negotiate to find and settle on a scale that does not compromise your operation. Know what you are willing to give and what you want to get, and just stay there!

People often think that the personality of a businessman or -woman must be rude, aggressive and almost arrogant. I believe, on the contrary, that success in business is realised when you are reasonable but purposeful, aggressive in intention but assertive in approach, with the ability to speak your mind in a manner that does not offend others and seeks to create an atmosphere of humour and positive energy around those you mix with in business. Ultimately, you want them to enjoy doing business with you.

Your capacity to take tough decisions

Successful businessmen and -women make decisions, easy or hard, in the interest of their businesses. If those decisions are delayed, they will compromise the bottom line. A decision to let go of a worker who is a liability to the business needs to be taken swiftly and promptly (of course considering the labour laws, which we will discuss at length in Chapter 12). Delaying that decision for one month will cost you a salary for which you will get no benefit.

Trust me, I have been a victim of this, and it has cost me dearly in business. I once employed a young boy because I knew the family and sympathised with their financial situation. Maybe that was a mistake in itself! It turned out that the boy did not have the same values as the family I knew. His work ethic was inexcusable, his attitude indefensible. I kept thinking about the family every time I had to take a logical and desirable decision. I confided in the father instead of confronting the boy. His father "fired" him from my business before I did.

The bottom line

Remember that business is about taking a risk for a reward. There is no point in doing it if it is not profitable. We are not talking about starting up an NGO, we are setting up a business, and a profit is what the business has to offer. You need to remember that there are various alternatives to starting and running your own business, for example:

1. earning a salary through formal employment, or
2. investing the money and earning interest and growth.

Although these options have their advantages and disadvantages (for instance, formal employment could require a qualification and experience which you might lack), the message is that they should be considered carefully before you venture into business. There is no point in entering into a business that will ultimately give you a return of R5 000 a month when you could be employed and earn R15 000. By the same token, there is no point in putting your hard-earned savings into a business to earn a return of 4% when you could be investing elsewhere at a rate of 7%.

Before you embark on a business venture, make sure that you are entering a profitable course that will generate the returns you are looking for.

There are various things that you need to anticipate here to assess whether this venture you are embarking upon will work for you and give you the financial results to which you aspire.

Return on investment

An estimate of your return on investment will indicate to you if the money you will put into your business will give you the rewards you are looking for. It is based on a simple calculation of the net profit (we will discuss this concept in the following chapters) as a percentage of the savings that you have generated over the years and invested into your business.

Example
Sam puts R30 000 into his catering business and anticipates that, after paying all his monthly bills and the running costs of his business, he will make

a net profit after tax of R1 500 a month or R18 000 a year. His return on investment is R18 000/R30 000 x 100 = 60%. By business standards, that is a good return on Sam's investment.

Your bottom line will be impacted on by a number of factors that we will discuss in the chapters that follow. At this point it suffices to alert you to the fact that unless your business provides better financial benefits than the alternative does, it is not worth entering into.

I think it is critical to note at this stage that, although the bottom line and the return on investment are key financial considerations for or against getting into business, there are numerous *non-financial* issues you may want to consider. The business may not offer you the profit or the returns that you are looking for, but may provide you and your associates with employment opportunities and an opportunity to make a contribution to society that fulfils your ethical desires. I have been running a business for the last three years that has not given me a cent in returns or profits. Apart from the fact that I am hopeful of its growth potential and that the trends suggest that the returns will surely come, the business employs more than 15 people in permanent positions. That, on its own, is motivation enough to keep running it.

Competition

A critical factor that we often fail to consider when deciding on business ventures is the extent to which competition can dilute our earning potential and even sink us. We often decide to enter into a particular kind of business because we like it. In fact, in many cases we do it because we have seen it working well for our friends and people we know, and we believe that it will be a safe and tested market, therefore we cannot fail. We do this without realising that those people have created a supplier base in the market that will increase consumer choices and dilute demand across the suppliers, thus reducing the prices and market share to our detriment.

Although venturing into a competitive environment is risky, it does not mean that you should not do it. All it suggests is that you develop a thorough assessment of the terrain to establish the following:

1. **The size and potential of the market for your commodities**

Sometimes you may find that the demand for certain commodities is well in excess of the supply; in other words, more people need more of a commodity than is available. Often people end up importing these commodities because the local market cannot meet the demand, or they resort to alternative commodities. These are the business ventures that you want to explore seriously, as they give you immediate space in the market to make money.

The opposite can also be true. You often find an influx of suppliers where the demand is not really that great. Getting into such a business is like setting yourself up to fail.

I am not suggesting that businesses that enter into a highly contested market are doomed to fail. As has been mentioned, a huge base of suppliers increases consumer choices, which invariably dilutes the potential of your business. But having made that statement, I want to note that there are many factors at play here. Right at the beginning of the book, I presented a diagram of the dynamics surrounding your business. Striking a right balance among these will lead to success, sometimes in the midst of steep, very steep, competition. The challenge in business is how to strike that balance.

In looking at the size of the market, we should not forget that South Africa is a global player and is generally well accepted in neighbouring countries. This creates a huge opportunity for our products to enjoy a market in Namibia, Zimbabwe, Swaziland, Mozambique and many other states. We often limit ourselves unnecessarily when we assume that we can play only in our local economies and not spread our wings more widely.

When I started my business consulting company, I never imagined operating outside KwaZulu-Natal, South Africa. I never explored avenues outside this space. Intensifying my research and striking the right business partnerships opened my eyes to the opportunities that existed for the business in the Eastern Cape, Gauteng and even outside South Africa's borders in countries such as Ghana and Namibia, where there is an even bigger demand for the services that the business has to offer.

2. The critical competitive criteria in the market

In light of serious and vibrant competition for the venture you are contemplating, you need to establish what the stimulus for the buying community is. In other words, you need to ascertain what the buyers respond to. Typically, buyers respond to the following:

COST, SERVICE EXCELLENCE AND QUALITY

You will often hear people saying, "I like buying at Joe Soap because they are cheap," or "I will never place an order with Tom Shank, because he takes a long time to deliver". Some will say: "Even though his prices are steep, I prefer him because his quality is good; you don't have to keep replacing his stuff." This basically gives you an indication of how players get sifted out from the market space because of their inability to satisfy the requirements of the market. Conversely, it also speaks to you of what to be careful about as you venture because that would be what the market wants.

The reality, though, is that the market will naturally want to balance out these factors. You will hardly find a scenario where buyers want the cheapest, irrespective of quality or delivery, or where they will buy an item because of its quality regardless of its exorbitant price. They know when to put on the brakes in their purchasing decisions and evaluate the other factors to eventually buy the right stuff! I believe that Mercedes-Benz customers, for instance, are less focused on price as they place more emphasis on quality and service, but they know when the price is unreasonable and will settle for less.

Studies that are continuously conducted on market trends can give you ideas of how to play with competition. There also are numerous market research companies that can assist you in studying these trends and behaviours.

3. Your competitive edge

Once you have assessed the market and its dynamics, it is vital that you establish where in the market you would have a competitive advantage over the other players. This assessment is particularly important because it will inform you upfront when you cannot play in this field because the competition will simply break you apart. Your competitive edge could be any of the following:

- your relationships in the market;
- your financial strength;
- your skills and expertise;
- your technology;
- your pricing structure; or
- your service offering.

Barriers to entry

One of the considerations as you decide on your venture is how easy or difficult it is for the average person to enter that particular field. It could be to your advantage if it is easy to get into your line of business and make money, but it could also be a serious disadvantage, as it increases the chances for competition both in the present and in the future. The easier it is for everybody, the more people will want to play in that market and the stronger the competition will be. As you make your assessment, some of the barriers to entry that you have to consider are *finance*, *approvals* and *skills*.

1. Finance

Some industries require huge investments to start and could be significantly unattractive to potential investors because of the risk involved. Think about how much money it would require to start a mining company and how much time it would take before you made your first rand of return. Consider tree planting, and how much you would have to put into the ground before you could smell profits.

The company I referred to earlier that is taking a long time to yield returns is a document management company. In simple terms, we keep documents on behalf of clients. The price to keep a bunch of documents in a box for a month is as low as R1.90. The investment that has to be made, however, is enormous. We have to have a warehouse that satisfies the requirements of the National Archives Act, is attractive and safe for the customers to trust, is adequately racked for ease of access to documents, and is equipped with the right security measures against fire and theft. Clearly, keeping boxes at R1.90 means that it will take a long time for the infrastructure to start paying for itself, which is a serious disincentive for most people. That is why there are so few of these companies around.

2. Approvals

There are businesses that do not have to go through rigorous certification and approval processes before they can be established and run. It is simply a case of starting and flying. Others, on the other hand, require many cumbersome applications, inspections, motivations and approvals before they can operate. The barriers are many, and many people will not make it into that space. The following are examples of approvals and certifications that you would require to succeed in certain fields:

- ❑ In the construction industry, government tenders require you to have CIDB (Construction Industry Development Board) and NHBRC (National Home Builders Registration Council) accreditation.
- ❑ Training services require SETA (Sector Education and Training Authority) and SAQA (South African Qualifications Authority) accreditation.

❑ Accounting services require SAICA (South African Institute of Chartered Accountants) and/or CFA (Chartered Financial Analyst) accreditation.

3. Skills

Some businesses require that you acquire the necessary skills and experience before they can make money. That could mean formal qualifications, as in the case of accountants, doctors, lawyers, engineers or architects. Anyone who wants to venture into these fields and compete successfully would have to have at least seven years' post-matric qualifications. This is a significant barrier and reduces your chances of fierce competition. In fact, this gives you a wonderful head start and you should accumulate more skills, more contacts, and more contracts.

Touching base with those in business

One of the things we often omit is to bounce our ideas off those who are already in the line of business we want to pursue. They will give you valuable information about the venture to which you aspire. They have made mistakes you can learn from, have faced challenges you will face as well, and have developed ways of doing things faster and more economically. You do not want to re-invent the wheel. Speak to them and learn. Beware, however, of speaking to potential competition. They may mislead you, either by discouraging you completely so that you end up not starting your venture, or by making you start off on a wrong path so that you face challenges and sink! The best advice is to contact people who are not in your direct space, for instance those operating in another province and not where you intend setting up your business.

It is advisable to seek employment in the kind of business you want to start. Make the sacrifice for your future and volunteer to help. In that way you will experience the practical side of your envisaged venture. Rotate right through the business in the course of your employment, getting the feel of finance, marketing, sales, the supply chain, and so on. Remember, at first you may have to do all these tasks yourself or have management oversight over them in your own venture. It is important to know how they work.

Spend time reading up about your line of business. Find the industry journals. Listen to interviews with people who are already there. They will tell you what the challenges are, what the pitfalls have been and what alliances and strategies you can develop in order to succeed. Just make sure you do not go into it blindly. Remember, failure in business costs a lot of money.

Bottom line – make sure that by the time you make the first move that costs money, you are certain that this is what you want to do!

Am I fit for business?

Take some time now to fill in the simple questionnaire below, which will give you an indication of the challenges that you will face in business and also help you assess whether you will be up to overcoming them. It is by no means a comprehensive guide to all potential business challenges but will certainly give you general indicators. Answer simply "Yes" or "No" in response to each question.

If you get a score of less than 60%, in other words, your "Yes" answers account for 60% of the questions asked, you may struggle in you own business and will have to work seriously hard to make it work. A score of 80% and above will indicate that you are a natural. I would go for it if I were you. The chances of success are great!

Remember, complete this questionnaire as honestly as you can. Avoiding the truth is merely deceiving yourself. Even if you decide to venture into business anyway, the questionnaire will help you to know your shortcomings and bring to the fore things to guard against as you proceed. Reflect honestly, and you will succeed.

BUSINESS SELF-EVALUATION QUESTIONNAIRE	YES	NO
Myself and business		
1. Am I a self-starter?		
2. Am I confident?		
3. Am I disciplined?		
4. Am I willing to live without an income?		
5. Am I ready to put in more time than the normal hours of work?		
6. Am I willing to sacrifice time with my family and friends?		
7. Am I creative?		
8. Do I like taking risks?		
9. Can I live with uncertainty?		
10. Can I work under pressure?		
11. Can I function under financial stress?		
My business and I		
1. Do I know all the dynamics of the business I intend venturing into?		
2. Do I have the skills to make it work in this line of business?		
3. Do I have effective support structures in this business?		
4. Do I have experience in the business I am pursuing?		
5. Can I satisfy clients?		
6. Can I perform multiple tasks?		
7. Do I have multiple business skills?		
The leader in me		
1. Would I readily take the decision to fire someone?		
2. Would I deny a free service or money to a relative or friend?		
3. Do I have what it takes to make people listen to me?		

4. Am I flexible in listening to other viewpoints?		
5. Can I give direction and monitor progress in what I need done?		
6. Am I a leader?		
7. Am I flexible in changing direction?		
8. Am I willing to push customers and clients for business and payment?		
9. Can I put pressure on suppliers and business associates?		
10. Am I competitive (positively)?		
11. Am I resilient and able to press on in times of adversity?		

Your score
Total score   29
Percentage

CHAPTER 4

Building a business model

- What will my business model look like?
- Who will be my customers?
- Who will supply me with the material/skills?
- Where will I produce the product?
- Where will the plant/offices be?
- How exactly will I do this?

A model of your business

In this chapter, we intend putting the pieces of the business puzzle together. You have hopefully decided, in principle, what type of business you want to open. Whether it be a security company, a consulting firm or a cotton-manufacturing plant, you know what you want. You have researched the market, spoken to those in business and confirmed that, if well run and managed, it is a business worth venturing into. Now is the time *really* to draw it up and conceptualise it. You now have to ensure that you can almost see the business working in your mind.

Business has many facets, all extremely important. Due consideration has to be given to all of them because they will, in balance, determine the success or failure of your venture. The diagram below depicts how all these facets will interrelate to build a successful business. Remember, they are all of great importance, and turning your attention away from one may have disastrous consequences for your success.

At this stage, although you have a real appetite for this business, you might just decide that the model has too many risks and weaknesses and is not worth pursuing. You will see during the course of this chapter that the pieces might not fall nicely into place and this would discourage you from venturing. Conversely, you will certainly have a good sense of which pieces to manage and get right in order for the entire business to succeed. You may, for instance, have a very good business concept but battle to find the right leadership and management for your business. Your task is to go out hunting, otherwise success is not imminent.

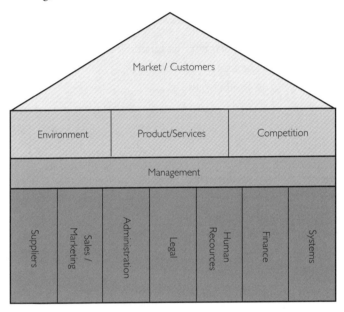

In a nutshell, your success will depend on the following:
- how you as a business person manage your customers, your product, your competition and the general environment around your business entity to guarantee your success, and
- how you manage the ingredients of your operation so that you are able to provide the right product to the right person at the right time and price. These ingredients will be: the supply chain, finance, sales, legal issues, your employees, technology and systems.

BUILDING A BUSINESS MODEL 47

You will notice from the diagram above that all these facets, whether in the external environment or internally, must be managed by you as the owner. It is up to you to employ management that will take care of these aspects, but, trust me, in the initial phase of your venture *you* will have to manage all of these one way or another. In this chapter, we will explore your product/service, your market/customers, your competition, the environment, and your management.

Before we dive into each one, remember that this is the stage when you draw up your business concept in greater detail. If the concept does not make sense to you, if the pieces do not give you the desired answers, then it certainly will not make sense to the funder. If each of these facets does not make sense and cannot be managed properly, consider pulling the plug and focusing on another venture!

Your product/service

You are getting into business with a product or service that you want to launch to make money. It is important that you know precisely what that product or service is. If you are vague about this central piece of your concept, you will fail to locate everything else in relation to your product. Let us look at some examples:

1. You want to enter the market with a cellphone shop that will sell but not repair cellphones and cellphone accessories; you do not want to open a business in communications.
2. You want to be a greengrocer and sell fruit and vegetables; you do not want to get into agriculture.
3. You intend making pallets and renting them out to businesses; you do not want to get into manufacturing other products.
4. You want to advise on tax issues and open a tax advisory service; you do not want to get into consulting.

I emphasise this point because I have interacted with a number of aspiring business people who were so vague that it took forever to figure out what it was that they wanted to do. If the product/service is not precisely defined, you will not be able to identify all the necessary variables that will attract costs and need to be managed. The product must be known and be identifiable, and all the people that you interact with must be able to locate your product in the range of related products.

Your market, your customers, must know what they will find when they enter your outlet. They must not be confused by advertising that creates expectations that lead to disappointment. They should not want you to repair their broken cellphones if you only sell new ones. More importantly, you should not accept broken cellphones for repair, because that is a completely different business model to yours; you will dent your image in business and lose future revenue.

I have an accountant friend who accepted a lucrative job to develop and implement policies for one of his clients. He knows how to do books, but does not have the skills and expertise to draw up a policy! To date, he has not been paid for the services rendered, because he ventured into an activity that is not in line with his business model.

Your market/customers

Once you have located and identified the product or service, you need to determine whether there is a market for it. The two fundamental questions that you are attempting to answer here are:

1. Will people be interested in my product or service?
2. What is the size of the market for my product or service?

These are critical questions, as they will determine whether or not you continue with your venture and how big it is going to be. Your personal interests must be put aside for a moment while you concentrate on the people out there. I may personally have a very strong liking for motorcycles, but that does not mean that everybody in Umlazi shares my passion and I can open a motorcycle business in Umlazi and make a killing! That market must be researched before I can commit to a business in that location.

People may be very interested in your concept, but their interest alone will not tell you whether there is a market. You also have to investigate their capacity to spend money on your product or service. The issues here are whether they have the *inclination* to spend money on your product or service, and whether they have the *purchasing power* to acquire what you will sell. Maybe what can give you guidance in this regard is Maslow's well-known hierarchy of needs, as depicted below:

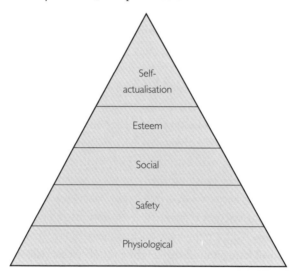

Maslow's theory suggests that people have sets of needs that they naturally want to satisfy before they can dedicate limited resources (i.e. money and time) to other needs. Differently put, an ordinary man would rather ensure that his family has shelter before he can buy them Christmas presents. This does not imply that he does not want to buy presents, but his logic is that he would rather they had a roof over their heads than that they play with toys in the rain!

That must give us some guidance in business. Using the example above, a toy shop would not be viable in a poor community simply because it is too high up in the hierarchy of needs. Let us look at this theory and explore the types of businesses we can set up, considering where people are in the needs hierarchy.

NEED	EXAMPLE	TYPE OF VENTURE
Self-actualisation	Truth, justice, wisdom, meaning	Library, Internet café, foreign exchange
Esteem	Self-respect, achievement, recognition, attention, reputation	Salon, publishing company, gym
Social	Friends, belonging, love	Restaurant, flower shop, gift shop
Safety	Medical, insurance, job security, financial reserves	Bank, stokvel, surgery, funeral parlour, building materials, security service
Physiological	Water, air, nourishment, sleep, shelter	Retail shop, agricultural produce, building material and implements

Maslow argues that the most important needs of society or people are the basic physiological needs: food, shelter, and so on. Once people have satisfied these basic needs, they increase their aspirations and develop another set of needs, elevated from the basic, such as the need for security and education. This will happen until they reach a set of self-actualisation needs, those of the rich and famous, who now aspire to actualise and develop unique identities and spend money on leisure, holidays, picnics, etc. This theory helps us in deciding what business to launch and where. For example, will it make business sense to open a Jet Ski business, executive restaurant or quad bike outlet in the middle of a rural village? Clearly you will not make money: as much as the residents would enjoy quad biking or jet-skiing or taking their families out to a nice buffet, they simply would rather spend their money on their basic needs. For example, they would rather save up for electricity at the end of the month. The concept is good; the market inappropriate.

As an entrepreneur, you should align your product or service to the target market, taking into account your assessment of their needs. Interact with the potential market. Make sure you understand exactly how people feel about the product you intend launching. You may even want to engage the services of a market researcher to do this analysis. Your primary question is, "Will my product or service sell in this market?"

Remember that the market is not necessarily geographically defined. In other words, setting up a business in Umlazi does not necessarily mean that I will be selling to or targeting the people of Umlazi. For example, if you look at all the gift shops in northern KwaZulu-Natal, they are not marketing to the people from Hluhluwe or Mtubatuba even though they are physically located there. They are, in fact, attracting middle- to upper-class tourist traffic, people in the social and self-esteem brackets of the hierarchy of needs. If this is the case with your business, that you have set it up away from your target market geographically instead of where it would ordinarily be visible to that market, you have a different challenge: how do you reach your market and attract sales? We will discuss this at length in Chapter 11: Marketing your business.

One of my associates has a retail outlet for biking accessories and even bikes right at the back of Pinetown, and is doing reasonably well. Trust me, his market is not Pinetown residents. He located his outlet just next to a quarry, which well-off people have identified as a nice hang-out where they gather with their quad bikes and motorcycles. Every weekend the place is packed with biking clubs and families from all over South Africa. They will need accessories such as helmets and spares because these vehicles will break down, and that is where he comes in with his business.

Your competition

Now you come to the uncomfortable part of your business design! You now know what product or service you will be selling. You have even identified who (the market) you will be selling to, and have done assessments to ascertain whether they would be willing and able to buy your offering. Now you have to contend with a serious challenge – you are not the only one! Someone else is already out there with the same idea, and others will enter sooner or later. How do you manage competition?

In a way we have dealt with this in the previous chapter, but unless you pin it down to the last degree, you will miss your fortune in the prevalence of stiff competition. You need to know who your competitors are, what they do and how you are likely to fare against them. This depends largely on the size of the market and what share you can win.

Size of the market

As discussed, you need to know the forces of demand and supply for your product or service. You need to know whether the market is already being tapped or not. You need to assess the size of the demand, the available supply and your potential competition. This is a very challenging and daunting task, but unless you can identify some gap in the market, you will go into business blindfolded. You need to establish whether there is a gap in supply that your offering can fill.

Again research surveys will give you guidelines. Talking around in the market will indicate to you where there are shortfalls in supply, where there is excess demand, where there is room for you to play. This, in essence, is when you do not directly fight competition, but get into untapped terrains. Fill the gap in the market. Increase the supply to match demand. This is probably a comfortable position to be in, as you are not creating business enemies but supplementing their supply. The question could be, "why were they not increasing their productive capacity to match the increasing demand?" but that is neither here nor there. Bottom line – you found a gap in the market and you swiftly filled it.

Your market share

A harder permutation is when you decide to be aggressive and take on the competition directly as you introduce your business. Here you are trying to win a share of the market, ordinarily taking it from existing suppliers or businesses. You will be faced with fierce competition. Your competitors will feel threatened and will employ every tactic they can to get you out of "their" space. Depending on their business ethics, they may even employ dirty tactics that you may be unaware of until it is too late.

The reality is that, being new in business, you have the odds stacked against you. The competition will have a huge advantage of time. They were there before you, have made the mistakes you are about to make, have found easier and cheaper ways of producing their products, and have developed technology and systems to make their production processes seamless. You still have to fiddle around until you get this right.

Of utmost importance is that they have built brands and embedded them in the market. The market knows of their existence and has tested their products and service delivery. Most have even signed long-term contracts that are almost impossible for customers to get out of. They have built relationships with the customer base. You will battle to break into the customer base and loosen their hold.

The good news is that despite these challenges, it is not an unachievable task. You will need to be strategic and systematically break through this wall. It may take time, but if you are persistent, you will make your breakthrough. Be very wary of growing too big, too quickly. Grow your market share in manageable chunks. Remember, Rome was not built in a day!

I entered an accounting field with well-known giants that I had to face. Maybe my advantage was that the market was bigger than the supply, so there was room for me to play with my company, Thabani Zulu & Co. But I also had to push my way through and demonstrate that there was a "new kid on the block". I had to convince the market that the skill set, delivery attitude and quality of product of my company would be a strong enough alternative to the known suppliers. In certain instances I had to push systematically for better recognition than my competitors, snatching every opportunity to demonstrate wealth of knowledge in order to take my rightful position in the market. Here are some tips that can help you to gain your market share:

1. *Work with the competition.* The big, established companies are always eager to partner with emerging ventures. They see it as some kind of social responsibility for which they will be acknowledged in the current

political climate. Use that to your advantage. Work with them for your growth and for introduction to their spaces, introduction to their contacts and building up a profile of your company.
2. *Follow the government mandate* and stay acceptable. At present there is much hype about Black Economic Empowerment (BEE) and BEE companies. Stay there. If you can employ women, the youth and people with disabilities, do so positively and purposefully. Let your venture earn mileage for being responsive to a call from government and society.
3. *Invest in business process improvements.* Customers look for product quality, service quality and cost efficiencies when they decide to purchase goods or services. Look and re-look at your production concept and streamline it with these aspects in mind. Study the competition and make comparisons. You should "pass" your concept only when you can demonstrate that you have achieved quality and efficiency, otherwise your competitors will make mincemeat of you.
4. *Establish your product niche*, whatever this might be. It could be your environmentally friendly production processes as opposed to those of your competition, the organic nature of your products, or the uniqueness of the product mix. It could be the dynamic nature and specialisation of your service team. Find that which differentiates you from the competitors and capitalise on it. Obviously, it must make sense to the market.

I hope that you have now assessed your competitors and how your business and products will fare against competition, and have developed in your concept a strategy to tackle them in the playing field. You are ready to move on with the design of your business concept.

The environment

South Africa is a legislated environment. There are too many do's and don'ts when it comes to business. The last thing you want is to be caught breaking the law and risking your business entirely. You cannot just open a liquor store or set up with gambling machines without the necessary licences from the liquor or gambling boards. By the same token, you cannot just start digging holes without the mining rights. All these actions will be violations that will cause you to be closed down immediately when they are discovered. This even includes setting up an operation in an area that does not have business zoning and is strictly zoned for residential purposes.

The point I am making is that you must familiarise yourself with the pieces of legislation pertaining to your business venture and ensure that you comply before you can take your concept further. You really do not want to be caught off guard when you apply for finance and the financiers send your application back to cover certain legislative ground before they can advance you the funds. At best you may embarrass yourself and demonstrate that you do not know what you are getting yourself into, thereby reducing the appetite of the financier to fund your venture.

Fulfilling the legal demands for the establishment of your venture has financial implications. Licences cost money. Approvals come at a fee. You need to be aware of what those costs are and build them into your concept. Even employment of people is legislated for, and there are minimum wage limits to which you must adhere. You must know these things and you must build them into your concept.

It is advisable to be in contact with a body that regulates the industry in which you intend setting up your venture. If you know a legal practitioner, do make contact with him or her and seek the necessary advice. You may even want to affiliate with a network of business people, for instance the Chamber of Business, so that you take advantage of the skills and expertise that are already in the network. The bottom line is that you want to be fully conversant with the legal requirements for your business to thrive.

Your management

The last thing, but certainly not the least important, to consider is how your business will be managed. Remember that businesses fail because they have inadequate management, are run almost by remote control and are not given direction and focus. If you intend applying for finance to get your business started, you had better make sure that you get this right! Finance houses are extremely particular about the people behind the business, what skills they have, and what experience they have gained over the years that would equip them to run a venture such as yours.

Realise that you may not be skilled in everything and that you will need help. I deal with this elaborately in Chapter 5: Choosing your partners, but it is critical to note that your business will require the following skills:

1. human resources;
2. marketing and sales;
3. finance and administration;
4. purchasing;
5. legal; and
6. information technology.

There is nothing that suggests that you need these skills in-house from day one. You can very well outsource some of these functions and pay specialists to implement certain things in your business and leave, to be called upon when required. You may want to call an IT specialist for a month to implement the necessary systems, for instance, instead of employing him or her full-time in your business. The point is, you must be able to tell when they have not given you what you require and protect your business against abuse.

The danger that we, especially small business people, fall into is to ignore these skills and pretend that we can do it all on our own. We see them as unnecessary, something to invest in when the business grows, forgetting that they are critical ingredients for the very growth to which we aspire.

The first step is to know your strengths and capitalise on them, saving your business money and not exposing it to abuse. If you know the law, for example, do not engage or employ a legal advisor, be one! It will cost you time and energy, granted, but that is the package of being in business: saving money and exerting energy. If you have partners, capitalise on their strengths. They have already taken the risk, they might as well go full out and make it work. Do not be bigger than your business and be the "boss" when you know you cannot afford to be. Roll up your sleeves and work hard at your business. It is your future, it is your pride!

CHAPTER 5

Choosing your partners

- What type of business will I set up?
- Who will my partners be?
- What will they bring to the business?
- How do I enter into contracts with them?
- What if they let me down?

In this chapter, I will explore the advantages and disadvantages of sharing ownership, control, risks and rewards in your business. I will also look at the pros and cons of various types of entity, thereby hoping to discourage the arbitrary and unscientific selection of business entity models. There has been a surge of CC and Pty registrations (these terms will be explained later) which are often not underpinned by any form of logic. Although entity registration has financial implications, this issue must not be viewed from a narrow financial standpoint only. The legal and future implications for the company have to be carefully considered.

Can you make it on your own?

This is a question only you can answer. I can merely give guidance to help you take a decision. There is absolutely nothing wrong with going into business on your own; in fact, it has many advantages over bringing other people into your venture. In this chapter we will examine the reasons behind taking a decision to partner, and also investigate different forms of business with their advantages and disadvantages. You have seen the dynamics of business in the previous chapter, where we discussed the business concept and what it will require to succeed. The question here is: do you on your own have what it will take to make your dream come true? If not, can you find ways of getting what you lack without necessarily bringing in partners? In other words, can you source the additional skills through contract arrangements with service providers and not through partnerships?

Something to keep in mind is that partnership in business is almost like marriage: although a "divorce" is possible, it is often very hard and painful, with emotional and financial implications. It is vital that you think thoroughly before you get into it. Make sure that it is what you want. I personally have had to endure the pain of breaking up a partnership because it was not what was best for business and for all partners concerned. Trust me, it was difficult for all of us. Do not let it happen to you if you can avoid it.

Can you afford not to have a partner?

I do not believe that there is one person who possesses skills in finance, human resources, IT, marketing and customer service in one. You may accommodate these functions in yourself initially for cost considerations, but sooner or later you will realise that you need people who specialise in these fields in your company, as indicated in the previous chapter.

The fact that you need these skills in your business does not mean that you should have partners who have them. There are accounting companies, legal firms, firms of architects and so on whose expertise can be sourced on an ad hoc basis as and when you need them, without having them permanently in-house. Do not fall into the trap of engaging them as partners when you need their skills for a limited period only.

As a matter of fact, I have realised that it is sometimes more advantageous to engage a marketing company to do your marketing than to have a full-time marketing person (partner or employee). It is easier to control the company by drawing up a delivery contract and just not paying them if they have not delivered. An employee, on the other hand, may sit around idly without getting much done and you still have to pay a salary at the end of the month. Your employee's laziness becomes your problem.

Partnership versus employment

You have the alternative of employing the skills you require in your business without having them as partners. This, once again, has its pros and cons, and the decision really is yours to take – I have already referred to some of the drawbacks of employing people. Partners are taking the risk with you and will not drain the business of funds while it is starting up, as they hopefully share a common vision with you. Employees, on the other hand, are not risk takers and are entitled to a monthly salary, thus putting pressure on you to sustain them.

Employees do not dilute your voice in the business and your capacity to take decisions and run with them, while partners have to be consulted in decisions and may not see things your way. This can be good or bad, depending on you as an individual. It may just be a good thing for your business to have partners, as they will keep you on your toes and cause you to give regular accounts of what you have done and the progress you have made. Remember, running a business requires personal drive, and having someone looking over your shoulder can enhance that drive. This choice between partnership and employment I will leave in your hands.

Choosing a partner

One of the biggest mistakes we make is selecting our friends as business partners. While there may be a lot of merit in such a choice, for instance personal trust and commitment to each other, love and empathy with each other's needs and comfort in being together, a partnership must have much more of a business focus. The selection of a partner is therefore not as easy as the selection of a friend. I have many friends who are not my business partners. Conversely, I have business partners with whom I have developed a friendship as we pursued business together, but who were not necessarily my friends at the start of the business.

The question that you need to ask yourself in this regard is, "What type of person does my business need"? This will help you identify the desired partner or partners. Businesses need people who can contribute one or more of the following:

1. Money

I will elaborate on this in Chapter 6: Financing your business. If your business requires funds, it is always advisable to identify an equity partner as it costs money to raise debt funding.

2. Skills

We have already discussed this. Skills are critical in business, and if you identify partners, you want to be careful that they complement you in this area. They can bring valuable ideas to the table and take your company forward.

3. Relationships

In loose terms we call these "contacts". Remember, you will be knocking on doors to generate business. Much of it, unfortunately, will be based on who you know and who knows you! This is the way of business, and as much as we want to fight it and call it names, we cannot wish it away overnight. Be wise and find people with "contacts" to be in business with.

4. Image

It is vital that you invest in the image of your business and associate it with people who have a positive profile in business and society. Can you believe how much business you would generate if Nelson Mandela were your partner? What message would you be sending to people out there? Look closely at your potential partner and quiz yourself on their profile or image. This can make or break your venture.

While the above factors are of critical importance, you should take care to choose a person with the same principles and ethics as yourself. You do not want to fight in the boardroom every day because your partner believes that a bribe must be paid to solicit business and you are against it. Or he wants the profits to be declared as dividends and you want to grow the business. Or she wants a part of that loan you acquired to buy nice cars, and you are adamant that it must all go into the business. You want to make this assessment about shared principles right up front and act on it before you end up with the wrong person in your company.

Forms of ownership

I have observed that small businesses tend to follow trends in setting up their structures. You find people registering close corporations (CCs) as if it is fashionable; everyone that I know has a CC! But if you ask why they chose a CC, you do not get a response that satisfies you. Then government preaches cooperatives, and everyone wants to have a cooperative. Ten people club together and register a cooperative simply because they hope to get government business. I really would like us to explore what these various entity types have to offer so that you can make an informed decision.

One of the first decisions that you will have to make as a business owner is how the company should be structured. This decision will have long-term implications, so consult with an accountant and attorney to help you select the form of ownership that is right for you. In making a choice, you should take the following into account:

- your vision regarding the size and nature of your business;
- the level of control you wish to have;
- the level of structure you are willing to deal with;
- the business's vulnerability to lawsuits;
- tax implications of the different ownership structures;
- expected profit (or loss) of the business;
- whether or not you need to reinvest earnings into the business;

- the business funding requirements; and
- your need for access to cash out of the business for yourself.

Let's look briefly at the various structures that are available to you: their nature, advantages and disadvantages.

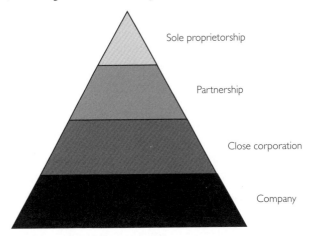

You will observe from the pyramid above that the forms of entities range from those that are very simple to start, run and manage (the sole proprietorship) to companies, which are very complex to set up and administer, with stringent regulations governing their operations and management.

A sole proprietorship

Sole proprietorships or sole traders are companies that are owned by one person, usually the individual who has the day-to-day responsibility for running the business. The individual owns all the assets of the business as well as the profits that are generated by it. Although this may be a good thing, it is important to note that the individual also assumes complete responsibility for any liabilities or debts that are incurred by his or her business. In actual fact, even legally and contractually there is no distinction between the business and the owner, and whatever happens in the business reverts back to the owner. Registration of the business with the banks normally just requires the owner's identity document.

You will see immediately that from a risk management perspective this is the riskiest form of business to run. For a start, the risks of the business are your personal risks. This is compounded by the fact that you have nobody to share that risk with.

Advantages of a sole proprietorship
- A sole proprietorship is the easiest entity to organise and to dissolve.
- A sole proprietorship is the least expensive form of ownership to set up. It requires the least administration.
- Sole proprietors are in complete control, and can take unilateral decisions. This form of business has the least bureaucracy.
- All income generated by the business belongs to the owner.

Disadvantages of a sole proprietorship
- Sole proprietors have unlimited liability and are legally responsible for all debts against the business. Their business and personal assets are at risk.
- Sole proprietorships are generally too small to attract lucrative investments and loans. The strength of the business depends on the strength of the owner.
- Sole proprietorships are generally too small to attract employees. People see these businesses as a risk, as they are generally in their start-up or growth phases.
- Sole proprietorships generally suffer from brain drain, as the owner carries the sole responsibility to grow and sustain the business.
- The life of the business is generally dependent on the life of the owner.

A partnership

A partnership is in essence two or more traders teaming up to form a joint business. It is no different from the sole trader in the manner in which the legalities are formulated and perceived. The banks and creditors are in essence dealing with the partners and not with the business, and their strengths become the acid test when the dealings are entered into. The law does not distinguish between the business and the owners.

Partnerships are regulated by an agreement between the partners. Drawing up an agreement is often left to the last moment, and yet it is the single most important document between the partners and becomes a reference when there are serious disputes between them. This legal agreement sets out how decisions will be made, profits will be shared and disputes will be resolved; how future partners will be admitted to the partnership; how partners can be bought out; and what steps will be taken to dissolve the partnership when necessary. Yes, it is hard to think about a break-up when the business is just getting started, but many partnerships split up at crisis times, and unless there is a defined process, there will be even greater problems. The partners must also decide upfront about matters such as how much time and capital each of them will contribute to the business.

Advantages of a partnership
- Partnerships are relatively easy to establish; however, time should be invested in developing the partnership agreement.
- With more than one owner, the ability to raise funds may be increased.
- The profits from the business flow directly through to the partners' personal tax returns.
- Prospective employees may be attracted to the business if given the incentive to become a partner.
- The business will usually benefit from partners who have complementary skills.

Disadvantages of a partnership
- Partners are jointly and individually liable for the actions of the other partners.
- Profits must be shared with others.
- Since decisions are shared, disagreements often occur.
- Some employee benefits are not deductible from business income on tax returns.

- The partnership may have a limited life; it may end upon the withdrawal or death of a partner.

A close corporation (CC)

A CC is the most popular form of business entity in South Africa. Maybe this is because it provides a balance between the legitimacy of a company and the flexibility and ease of formation of a sole proprietorship or partnership. CCs are very easy to register and do not cost much, yet they are viewed and respected as authentic business entities, removing some legal risks from the members or owners. They have to be registered and run in accordance with the rules of the Close Corporations Act.

Advantages of a CC
- Registration is simple and less costly than that of a company.
- CCs are easier to run and manage than companies. The requirements for their administration are less stringent.
- Distributions of income to members by a CC are exempt from income tax.
- CCs enjoy the status of legal persons and can be legally dealt with separately from their members.
- Liability of members for the debts of a CC is limited.
- Owners' interest is not limited to capital. A member can have a greater interest in the business than their proportionate share of capital injected.

Disadvantages of a CC
- CCs are taxed as if they are companies. The rate of tax for a company is normally higher than that of an individual.
- CCs are limited to ten members. This could prove to be a limitation to the growth of your business.
- The actions of the members of a CC can bind the CC and other members.
- Members in a CC can, however, be held personally liable if it can be proved that they acted negligently and without due care.

- CCs need to keep formal documents of their registration and affairs to remain reputable.
- It is impossible to sell a CC to a company or to make it a subsidiary of a company or part of a group structure.

Important legislative changes on CCs

The new Companies Act that comes into effect in 2010 provides for the phasing out of close corporations. This means that no new CCs will be registered once the Act is promulgated. If you already have a CC, it can continue to trade until deregistered, dissolved or converted into a private company, which I will discuss later. You can, however, elect to convert your CC into a private company at any point. The reason for the phasing out of CCs is simply that if a private company were regulated in such a way that it was not subject to strict financial reporting and auditing requirements, it would, in essence, have similar characteristics to a CC. This does not justify having a separate legal entity.

A company

A company is the sum total of efforts (monetary and physical) by individuals, but unlike a partnership it has a life of its own separate from its constituent parts. The owners surrender their rights and obligations to the entity in as far as its business operations are concerned. A company can be taxed, it can be sued, and it can enter into contractual agreements. The owners are its shareholders. The shareholders elect a board of directors to oversee the major policies and decisions, because the company has a life of its own and does not dissolve when ownership changes.

Advantages of a company
- Shareholders have limited liability for the company's debts or judgments against the company.
- Generally, shareholders can be held accountable only for their investment in shares held at the company. (Note, however, that officers can be

held personally liable for their actions, such as the failure to withhold and pay employees' tax.)
- Companies can raise additional funds through the sale of shares.
- A company may deduct the cost of benefits it provides to officers and employees.
- A company can choose the status it prefers, from being a limited company to a limited and unlisted company, and to a limited listed company. This enables it to attract investors and dilute risks.

Disadvantages of a company
- The process of incorporation requires more time and money than for other forms of organisations.
- Companies are regulated by the Companies Act and are monitored by national, provincial and local agencies. As a result, they may have more paperwork to deal with in order to comply with regulations.
- Incorporation may result in higher overall taxes. Dividends paid to shareholders are not deductible from business income, thus they can be taxed twice.

Important legislative changes on companies

The new Companies Act that I referred to earlier, which regulates phasing out of CCs, further provides for the formation of two types of companies, namely profit and non-profit companies. Your business is likely to fall into a category of private "profit" companies or personal liability "profit" companies. In these categories you can still be the only director or shareholder in your profit company and, unlike before, you can have more than 50 shareholders. The transferability of shares will still be restricted, and a private company will still be prohibited from offering shares to the public.

The governance of private companies will be less stringent. For instance, the company will not be expected to have a company secretary, an auditor or an audit committee unless it wishes to do so. Further, small private companies will be relieved of stringent audit requirements. It is important to note that although this will no longer be a requirement, it still remains good business practice. Further, the company may be compelled by banks and other trading partners to have a set of audited financial statements.

I hope that this discussion has helped to give you a clearer idea of what type of business entity you want to set up. Remember, although you want to solve the problems now and make sure that you get your business going as soon as possible and at the lowest possible price, you need to keep your future requirements in mind. You do not want to register a business that will limit your future growth. Moreover, you want to look at a business that will balance your risk and return potential. You want to protect yourself adequately as an individual against the risks that your business will face. You may have a family as well, and you do not want to expose them unduly to the risks that you will encounter in business.

CHAPTER 6

Financing your business

- How much do I need to start my business?
- Where can I find the money?
- What will financiers need from me?

There is no point in going into the discussions in this chapter if you have not done the exercise of modelling your business as outlined in Chapter 4. Often we dive into issues of raising finance and approaching banks and want to see money in the business accounts before we even think about how the business will be modelled. This makes potential investors and funders sceptical of us and our businesses because the concept is not sound.

The common saying that it costs money to make money is very true in business. If you are not prepared to spend money, you will not make a success of your business. Businesses needs equipment, premises, vehicles and people. All of these will be engaged in order to conduct activities for which you will charge your clients and make a profit, but they must be acquired at some cost.

In this chapter we will explore various ways of raising money for your business. We will initially look at mechanisms for raising start-up capital, and then examine expansion financing for your company.

Where can I find money to start my company?
Almost every person that I have interacted with is grappling with this question. People have brilliant ideas that they want to put into practice, but are limited by a lack of funds. "Start-up capital", they call it! Well, where can this come from?

There are two primary sources of business finance that we will explore in this chapter, namely equity and debt, each with its pros and cons.

Equity financing

Using equity finance is probably the cheapest way of starting up a company. Equity includes the savings you have put aside over time, donations from your relatives and friends, the retirement or pension money that you have earned from your previous employment: in other words, any money that comes out of *your* pocket.

The wonderful thing about equity finance is that it is *your* money and you can do with it what you want. You do not have anyone looking over your shoulder and dictating or criticising your decisions in business. You do not have to account to others. You have put your own money at risk, and you can manage it as you see fit.

The other advantage is that, unlike debt financing, which we will discuss shortly, equity finance does not attract administration costs and interest. Remember that those who advance money to you are also in business. They have to make money out of you! Running your venture out of equity would therefore cost you a lot less than financing your business with borrowed funds. We will illustrate this shortly when we discuss debt financing.

You need to be mindful that business is taking a risk for an unknown but anticipated reward. If things go sour and you had put in your own money, you cut your losses and go! Bad as it is that you have suddenly lost your hard-earned savings, that is about all you will lose financially. If the same happens in the case of a debt-funded business, however, you have to contend with the funders who want their money and will explore all possible avenues to get it back. Actions include: listing you on the credit bureaus, filing for liquidation of your business, and looking at your other personal assets with a view to selling them to raise the outstanding money. You will have to engage legal experts at extra cost to try to protect yourself against these losses. Times will be hard.

The reality about equity financing, though, is that it is hard to come by. Very few people have money floating around with which to start up businesses. You will hear that the whole world is in a financial slowdown, and therefore few have money to spare. You probably do not have any spare money either. Chances are that you do not have the funds readily available to kick-start your venture. Trying to raise this kind of money will be a long and painful process, and you may even miss a perfect opportunity because you are still trying to raise the funds. It is not always a practical option, although desirable. One way of getting around it, as we discussed in Chapter 5: Choosing your partners, is to find someone who can contribute their equity to your partnership, thereby avoiding having to raise bank loans to start your venture.

Debt financing

Debt financing means that you bring in a third party, often a bank or other financing institution, to put money on the table for you to start a business. We will discuss these financing structures in some detail. The financiers will advance you the money and, as in the case of buying a car, request that you pay this off in instalments over an agreed timeframe, and during that timeframe they will be asking for their cost of capital or interest. Let's illustrate this with a simple example.

> Kate wants to start a catering company, and a bank agrees to give her a loan of R100 000. The following will happen.
> 1. The bank will charge an administration fee to draw up the papers and will add the charges to their systems, say R1 000. Immediately she has a debt of R101 000 in order to have R100 000 to start her company.

2. Kate and the bank will agree on a period over which she will repay the money, say five years, and the interest they will charge on the loan, say 10%.
3. Every month for the next 60 months (or five years), Kate will have to pay the bank an amount of R 2 124,70.
4. At the end of the five years Kate will have paid (R2 124,70 x 60) = R 127 482,27 for a R 100 000 loan, an additional amount of over R 27 000. In essence, Kate is paying an average of R 458,04 per month just for having asked for a loan of R 100 000, and she will pay this every month for five years. If she asks for a loan of R 200 000, this amount doubles to over R 900 per month.

What are the considerations with debt finance?

Cost of debt

A serious consideration is how much will it cost you to raise this kind of money. You have seen in Kate's example that it will cost her R 27 000 in total or R458 per month for five years just in interest to service a debt of R100 000. Because this cost has to be built into the cash flows of the business, you will need to ensure that the business is able to service this debt. The determining factors in this transaction are:

1. the amount of the loan required, including the administration fees and any other fees that will be charged by the financial institution;
2. the interest rate; and
3. the period over which the loan will have to be paid back.

What is of critical importance is to find out what the instalments per month will be for your loan, given the agreed-upon interest rate and the period of the loan. This can be a cumbersome calculation and would be easier with a financial calculator. In any event, the financing institution will do it for you and ensure that you accept it at the point of granting the finance. I have, nevertheless, given you a guideline for calculating this amount in the Repayment Calculator that appears in the Appendix at the end of this book. Let's look at two extracts from the table in the Appendix below.

Example 1
If you were loaned R300 000 by the bank at a rate of 13% to repay over 36 months, your repayments would be approximately:

R300 000 x 0.03369 = R10 107 per month.

(Look at 13% in the "interest rate": column going down and 36 in the "number of months" row going across to find the factor of 0.03369, which you multiply by the loan amount of R 300 000 requested.)

NO. OF MONTHS	INTEREST RATE				
	10%	11%	12%	13%	14%
35	0.03306	0.03353	0.03400	0.03448	0.03496
36	0.03227	0.03274	0.03321	0.03369	0.03418
37	0.03152	0.03199	0.03247	0.03295	0.03343
38	0.03081	0.03128	0.03176	0.03224	0.03273
39	0.03014	0.03061	0.03109	0.03157	0.03206
40	0.02950	0.02998	0.03046	0.03094	0.03143
41	0.02889	0.02937	0.02985	0.03034	0.03083
42	0.02832	0.02879	0.02982	0.02976	0.03025

Example 2
If you were loaned R1 million by the bank at a rate of 15% to repay over 60 months, your repayments would be approximately:

R1 000 000 x 0.02379 = R23 790 per month.

(Look at 15% in the "interest rate" column going down and 60 in the "number of months" row going across to find the factor of 0.02379, which you multiply by the loan amount of R1 million requested.)

NO. OF MONTHS	INTEREST RATE					
	13%	14%	15%	16%	17%	18%
55	0.02423	0.02474	0.02525	0.02577	0.02630	0.02683
56	0.02391	0.02442	0.02494	0.02546	0.02599	0.02652
57	0.02361	0.02412	0.02463	0.02516	0.02569	0.02622
58	0.02331	0.02382	0.02434	0.02487	0.02540	0.02594
59	0.02303	0.02354	0.02406	0.02459	0.02512	0.02566
60	0.02275	0.02327	0.02379	0.02432	0.02485	0.02539

The table in the Appendix covers interest rates of 10% to 20% with loan repayment periods of 1 month to 60 months. Use a financial calculator or consult a financial advisor to find the factors for loans that exceed these parameters. The idea is that you need to be aware of what your repayments on the loan are going to be before you lock yourself into the agreement.

Commencement date

You should be very mindful of when the finance house requires you to start repaying the amount advanced. Careful consideration should be given to how much time you will need to set up your venture, when you will effectively start servicing your first customer, and how much time it will take for your business to start making money. Your commencement of the repaying of the loan should be timed with due regard to all of the above. Remember, as you wait with the repayments, the interest clock is ticking and it is effectively costing you more and more, so your set-up processes should be very quick to avoid unnecessary cost of capital.

Most finance houses will give you this grace; use it wisely, and do not abuse it by delaying starting up your business and generating revenue to start servicing this loan.

The period of the loan

Keep in mind that if you enter into a debt contract, you are locked into it until the debt is fully paid up. Look carefully at this period before you enter into any binding agreements. Scientifically, the longer the period, the more you will have paid in interest by the time it expires, but the less strained your cash flow will be, making it easier for your business to operate. Do you want to have an easier cash flow from the start, or would you rather discharge your obligations and be debt free as soon as possible? It is a difficult question to answer, and the choice will depend on your financial projections and the degree to which they materialise. My advice is: pay as much as you can afford and do not deprive your business of financial resources to operate.

Let's consider this example:

If Mr Msomi borrows R100 000 and contracts to pay it back over 12 months at 14% interest, his repayments will be R100 000 x 0.08979 = R 8 979,00 per month. If he extends this period to 24 months, the repayments reduce to R100 000 x 0.04801 = R 4 801,00, giving him monthly savings of R 4 178,00 but prolonging the repayment period. What makes sense for Mr Msomi in his specific circumstances will essentially be for him to decide.

The contract

One of the mistakes we make is to sign the contract agreements in haste and in the excitement of knowing that we have been funded and can start realising our dreams in business. Always remember that this money is not a gift and will have to be paid back, otherwise there will be severe consequences in your private life. Read the contract terms and conditions very carefully. Understand what the financier wants from you and assess whether you are able and willing to offer what they require in exchange for the money to start your venture. Some of the typical things financiers require are:

1. That you sign personal surety for the amounts advanced. This means that in the event that your business cannot pay the amounts due, you, in your personal capacity, will repay the debt.
2. That you cede of your investments or cover on your life. Such cessions would give guarantees to the bank or financier that, should anything happen to you, they would have the first claim on your cover, even ahead of your family members.
3. That you provide collateral or some form of security against the loan, for instance some of your personal assets. These could be movable assets on which you do not owe anything, which you can cede to the financier in the event that you are unable to repay the amounts due.

The financing institutions

In South Africa there are various institutions that can provide you with finance. This finance can take several forms, as we will discuss shortly. Each of the financing institutions has its own criteria, and you have to examine their criteria very closely against your own requirements and the nature of the business you intend opening. Below is a list of these financing institutions. The list is not exhaustive. You can search on the internet or contact your financial advisors for information about other institutions that can offer you finance, and their requirements.

- Commercial banks:
  Absa;
  First National Bank;
  Nedbank; and
  Standard Bank;
- Ithala Finance Corporation;
- Business Partners;
- KZN Growth Fund;
- National Youth Development Agency;
- Land Bank;

- Industrial Development Corporation (IDC); and
- microfinance lending organisations.

What types of finance are available?

Different institutions will offer different packages, and it is difficult to speculate about what you will find out there. Some are rigid in their offering and will offer packages that are fairly generic, while others have strong business finance divisions and will tailor their packages to suit your needs. The best is to shop around for a financing institution that will listen to your requirements and make attempts to satisfy them. Let's discuss some of the types of finance that are available to you.

1. Asset finance

This type of finance is for the acquisition of assets, e.g. buildings, vehicles, equipment and machinery. It is regarded as the safest form of finance for the banks, as it has an underlying asset. If you are unable to repay your debt, the banks will have recourse to the asset that they financed, and can repossess it and sell it on the open market. They will generally keep title over the asset or own it until it is fully paid up.

Financing institutions look very closely at the risks associated with the particular asset when they grant this type of finance. For instance, is it a specialised asset that will be difficult to sell? How quickly does it lose value as it is used? And so on. They will structure the loan, interest rate and period based on their assessment of risk associated with the asset and with your business.

2. Working capital finance

This is, in essence, finance to enable you to start your operations. Financing institutions realise that businesses do not generate returns immediately when they are launched: they need some money to buy the initial stock, make security deposits on business premises, and maybe even pay salaries for a certain period before money can be generated by the business itself.

These loans are unsecured and are generally risky for the bank and for your business. You do not want to run your business with loan funding. If it is as good as you want it to be, it should run with its own money. Try to keep loan finance as low as possible by making personal sacrifices along the way. If you can reduce the operational expenses by cutting out any unnecessary luxuries, do so. It will benefit your business in the long run. Go for smaller premises, try to do certain things yourself instead of employing people, buy minimal stock, and so on. Do not burden your business with unnecessary loans!

3. VAT finance

You will understand this better after reading the section on value-added tax (VAT) in Chapter 15. For now, let us just understand that what you will be purchasing as you start your venture has VAT built in. For example, if you buy a van for your operations for R180 000, you will be charged as follows:

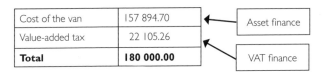

Cost of the van	157 894.70
Value-added tax	22 105.26
Total	**180 000.00**

Asset finance

VAT finance

In a nutshell, how does this work? The R22 105,26 that you paid to the supplier of the van is payable to the South African Revenue Service (SARS) by the supplier, who will put this amount on his return and pay it over to SARS. If you register your business for VAT (which is also covered in Chapter 15), you will claim this money back from SARS.

4. Leasing

Another option that you have for financing the start of your business is leasing. Remember that a substantial amount of the required capital will usually be for purchasing assets. With this financing strategy you do not, in fact, purchase the equipment, computers or vehicles, but lease them. Many organisations, e.g. Nashua and Olivetti, will lease the equipment to you and take it back after a period. By then you would have built up your business sufficiently to purchase your own equipment. Be careful, though, of how those deals are structured – they can be quite expensive in the long run. They are, however, an option available to you.

5. Factoring of invoices or debtors

This practice is becoming very popular in South Africa. There are institutions that make money from buying debtors' books at amounts less than the value of the debts. They then assume the responsibility and risk for collecting from the debtors and retain a premium for themselves. For instance, if Mr Mnguni owes you R120 000, you can sell that debt for, say, R100 000 to a debt collection agency. They pay you R100 000 to use in your business and they take the risk of collecting the debt from Mr Mnguni. If they succeed, they will make R20 000 from the transaction. The risk is theirs if they fail. You will need to be careful, though, because the debtors are your clients. You do not know how uncomfortable they might be with the mechanisms used by the collection agency to recover the outstanding amounts. It is advisable to have a strategy in your company of handing over only those clients with whom you will never have a relationship again anyway, in order to avoid spoiling future business relations. Do not go around selling current clients to recover your money!

An even safer alternative is that offered by the banks. They have realised that clients do take time to pay, and they buy invoices. Basically the bank will assess your debtors' book for probability of recovery. If they believe that the debts are recoverable in time, they offer finance against the book. You will obviously be paying interest until the debtor pays you, then you can settle with the bank.

6. Government grants

This is the type of finance that you should grab with both hands when it comes your way. It becomes available when government identifies a sector of need and wants to support it through grants and subsidies. This is free money to you and can go a long way to helping you create and sustain your business. It must be used very wisely, however, and not squandered.

Some tips about financing your business

A loan is not a gift!
Always remember that finance, particularly loan finance, has to be repaid to the institution in the future. Do not treat it as a gift and abuse it. It has severe cash-flow implications for your business and it can lead to draining legal battles between you and the financier if not paid back. Most agreements place even the burden of the legal fees on you in the case of non-payment of the monies due to the financier. You really do not want to land yourself in such a situation.

Equity is better than debt
Where possible, try for equity rather than debt financing. It will introduce an equity participant into your venture as we have discussed, but maybe it will also enhance discipline and accountability. It may keep you in check to know that you have a partner in your venture who has an interest in its success. Because she is placing her money at risk, your business does not have to commit cash flows to repay debt. If you can put your own money into the business, by all means do so. After all, it is your business, your concept, and you must trust it enough to risk your own money before you can expect someone else to do so.

Start small and grow big!
Be practical and lean in your financing of the venture. Do not aim too high and apply for loans that the business may not be able to afford to pay back. Assess your immediate and pressing requirements and apply for those to be met. Try to make the business generate its own wealth and grow systematically from there. You really just want to reduce the debt burden to the bare minimum possible. Get smaller premises, do not invest in lavish furniture, employ skeleton staff, pay practical salaries, purchase reasonable machines and equipment. Make sacrifices. You are investing in your future here, and you need to make sacrifices. There is no point in showing off with material possessions when your business is strained. Now that is coming from an expert who has paid the price – dearly! You are not a millionaire yet. That is your aim, not your current reality. Do not fool yourself.

Believe in your business plan

We will discuss the business plan in the next chapter, but do not draw up a business plan merely to bluff the financier. It will not work in the long run. Trust your plan yourself as if you were going to be risking your own money because, in the final analysis, you will be. Test it for risk and ensure that you are covered.

Make sure you can afford the repayments

Structure the finance so that it is manageable for the business. You may want to extend the time to repay the loan. As you have seen, this will increase the interest you will pay in the long term, but it will minimise your cash-flow commitments and allow the business the growth it requires. Negotiate the rates. Do not just grab anything that the financiers offer you because you are desperate to start your business. They are in business as well, and they will want to make money out of you. Keep a cool head and take your time.

CHAPTER 7

Buying an existing business

- To buy or not to buy?
- How much should I pay for a business?
- How best do I make it work?
- How do I raise finance for it?

In Chapter 4 we dealt with the art of modelling and creating a business in your mind. Often we ignore the fact that the model exists and has been tested. We force ourselves to reinvent the wheel. My advice is: before you launch yourself into creating a new business, you need to research the viability of the option to buy an existing business and the benefits of doing so.

Does buying an existing business make sense?

Buying an existing business has its advantages and disadvantages. It is a decision that has to be carefully considered. It is vital that you consult experts in this area before you get yourself into a transaction that does not make sense in the long run.

Starting up a business, as you are probably aware, is a strenuous and daunting task. It is extremely risky and time-consuming, and requires numerous assessments. It is risky not only for you, but also for the financing institutions, your customers and your employees.

1. The financing institutions have not seen your concept in action; they are not sure whether it will fly and are sceptical of putting their money into it.
2. Your customers are dealing with your business for the first time. They are not sure whether it is perhaps a fly-by-night operation and they will lose out on guarantees because it will not be there the next day.
3. Your employees are not sure whether their salaries will be sustained by the business in the long run or they will find themselves jobless without anywhere else to go.

Everybody is sceptical of a new business, for genuine reasons, and it will take a lot of courage, perseverance and vigilance to launch a new concept in the market and succeed in it. It is certainly not for the faint-hearted.

Buying something that already exists, on the other hand, provided it is done with insight and makes business sense, is a much wiser alternative to starting something new. The market is known and stable, the systems are in place, the infrastructure is up and running and the business has built a history of revenues and expenditures, therefore the assessments are easier and less risky. It is a less painful exercise by a serious margin. My advice would be to try to find something that is already there rather than kill yourself by starting afresh.

But, hey! That is just me! Someone else might think differently. It is the very challenge that intrigues them, the thrill of the unknown. They would be more committed to their own brainchild than to someone else's idea. They might argue that it would enable them to configure their businesses the way they want to rather than having to face the pain of rearranging something they have adopted. I do not even want to dispute those valid arguments. Maybe I am being too personal in my thinking. I started two businesses from scratch and I am not about to face that challenge again. It has taken a lot of my personal strength to see them through – I am exhausted and would rather use someone else's brain to launch me into another venture. If you have the energy to embark on a new venture, however, go for it. Just do it wisely!

What must you know before you buy?

Buying an existing business is not just a case of having money, liking something that someone does, and acquiring it. You will lose that money! You must proceed cautiously, and certain questions must be answered to your satisfaction before a decision is taken.

Why is the seller selling?
People sell for different reasons. Some sell because they are emigrating to join their families elsewhere; others sell because they have just got married and want to be with their spouses in another city; still others have newborn babies and want to devote their attention to the little ones. Some sell because they are fatigued and want to retire; they have been doing this for too long and are bored. Or they sell because they want to consolidate their business portfolio, and this business does not fit the profile. They have genuine reasons for selling.

On the other hand, some will sell because their product is losing space in the market, because there are advancements in the market that throw them out of place. Or they sell because they have lost a significant customer and will be out of business anyway. They sell because their concept is expensive to run and does not generate profits for them. Perhaps they want to sell because they find the competition too frustrating. Sellers could have any of these reasons, but they might just not tell you lest it discourage you from buying!

How is the business doing?
Once you know where the seller is coming from, your next set of questions will be around the business. You want to know what the business formula is. What makes people want to come to this particular business? If it is their relationship with the seller, will they support a new owner? Is the product slowly being pushed out of the market by new inventions, or is there still ample room to exploit the market with this product?

Can the business still grow?
Remember, buying a business is buying future profitability. If the business is priced right, at neither a premium nor a discount, it goes without saying that it must realise profits that will exceed the purchase price, otherwise there is no sense in investing in it.

You therefore have to quiz yourself thoroughly on the growth potential of the business you are buying. Is there room for growth? Do the premises provide sufficient room for expansion? Is the market not saturated? Even more important: what will the business need to grow? Does it, in fact, need you? Does it need a new profile, new management, or new systems?

These are very practical questions, and you will need to be very honest in answering them. You cannot afford to base your decision on emotion and your liking of the business and what it will represent when you acquire it, only to regret it down the line. Because we are under pressure from society to be seen to be successful, we occasionally take such decisions blindly and without asking these critical questions.

Why do I want to buy this business?
The "why" is another blunt question you will need to engage with in your quest to purchase a business: is it because of its viability that you want to buy it, or are you motivated by an attachment to the product it sells?

One of my associates is involved in training and conducts a number of training courses around the country. His quotations for training always included printing costs for the packs of course material, which he used to outsource to printing companies at exorbitant amounts. He later realised that it made sense for his business portfolio to purchase a printing company and use it primarily to print his training material. Over and above the existing clients of the printing company, he brought one additional client immediately, namely himself. He also managed to cut the profits that the printing company previously made from him and reduced his costs of providing training, thus realising more profits in his training venture.

You therefore need to know why you are buying this business so you can have a strategy once the purchase and sale have gone through. You will need to capitalise on your reasons for buying this business, and make it work.

The financial statements

Before we look at how you can attach a price to the business you intend buying, we need to understand the basics of business financial administration. There are four critical financial documents that I want to introduce at this stage.

Balance sheet

Every business has, or at least should have, a balance sheet. This is a statement or document of a business's financial position at any given time. It is sometimes referred to as a statement of assets and liabilities, and that is precisely what it is – a statement of the business's assets and its liabilities.

This statement details what the business owns (vehicles, land, equipment, plant, etc.) and attaches rand values to these. It then details what its liabilities are (money owed by the business to the creditors, the banks, SARS, etc.), also with their values. The result of this, i.e. assets less liabilities, is the equity that is sitting in the business for owners. A typical balance sheet would look like this:

BALANCE SHEET OF ALMA TRADERS AS AT 31 DECEMBER 2009		
EQUITY AND LIABILITIES	Note	
Retained earnings	1	120 000
Liabilities	2	620 000
		740 000
ASSETS		
Fixed assets	3	500 000
Current assets	4	240 000
		740 000

1. The *retained earnings* is the equity or net worth of this business. It actually represents the amount of money that the owners have accumulated thus far in the business. It does not necessarily have to be cash in the bank; it may be locked up in the assets of the business and could be realised in cash if the assets were to be sold and the liabilities paid.

2. As explained above, *liabilities* are the amounts that the business owes to various people. This represents the amount that other people have a claim to. If the owners wanted their retained profit in cash, they would first have to settle the liabilities by selling assets.
3. *Fixed assets* are assets that last longer than a period of 12 months in the business and are typically not easy to convert to cash, e.g. the buildings, the plant, equipment and vehicles.
4. The *current assets*, on the other hand, are more fluid and easily convertible to cash or are cash, e.g. the amount in the bank, the stock and the debtors of the business.

What we need to take from this discussion is that, in a nutshell, the balance sheet gives the net value or worth of the business. Keep this thought for future discussions.

Income statement

The income statement represents the financial performance or trading of the business. It gives you information about how the business is doing out there in the market. Is it making profits or losses, and how are its costs structured? A typical income statement would look like this:

INCOME STATEMENT OF ALMA TRADERS FOR THE PERIOD ENDING 31 DECEMBER 2009		
	Note	
Turnover	1	930 000
Less: Cost of Sales	2	600 000
Gross Profit	3	**330 000**
Plus: Other Income	4	15 000
Gross Income	5	**345 000**
Less: Operating Expenses	6	250 000
Net Profit	7	**95 000**

1. *Turnover* is the amount that the business is making from invoicing or billing its customers. In other words, it is how much the customers have

paid or will pay for the services rendered or goods sold, excluding value-added tax (VAT), which we will discuss in Chapter 15.
2. The ***cost of sales*** relates to the amounts expended directly in making the sales. In other words, how much money did it cost to make the sales? If you are in the IT business and you sell computers, this would be the purchase price of the computers sold. Likewise, if you were manufacturing detergents, it would be the total cost of the raw materials used in sold detergents, the cost of electricity used, the labour used and other overheads expended to make available the detergents that you sold.
3. ***Gross profit*** is the return made from the sales, excluding the other costs of running your business. It assumes that you have no other costs other than those directly associated with the sales.
4. ***Other income*** relates to income generated by your business but not associated with your core business concept. For example, if you had surplus cash that generated interest for you in the bank, this interest would then be your other income.
5. ***Operating expenses*** are costs associated with running your business but not with making sales: the administration costs, the marketing expenses, the rental of the office space, and so on.
6. ***Net profit*** is, therefore, the total earnings that the business generated when all was said and done. That is the return to the owners. Remember that this is then, in theory, the taxable income on which SARS would be basing their entitlement. We will discuss this issue in greater detail in the section on income tax in Chapter 15.

Budgets and forecasts

Every businessman and -woman must think ahead. We will discuss the art of thinking ahead in Chapter 9. This is articulated in the budget, a document that spells out what the projected financial structure of the business will look like. It would typically project the income, expenses and present quantum of the profits and losses that the business will sustain over the planning period. Let's leave the budget at this point and deal with it comprehensively at a later stage.

Management accounts

These would vary in presentation and disclosure but generally follow the principles of the income statement and balance sheet, only they are presented more frequently than these annual statements. They assist management in understanding on a regular basis, generally monthly, how the business is operating, in order to be able to take quick business decisions before it is too late.

Management accounts reflect a properly managed business. They indicate that managers are keeping tabs on the business operation and are constantly challenging themselves to take better decisions based on the outcomes of their past pronouncements on the direction of the business.

Now that we have a sense of some of the financial information that businesses generally present, I believe we can go on and attempt to attach a value to the business you intend buying. Remember, there will be a huge difference in position between you and the seller, where you must want to pay the lowest price possible for the business while he will be shooting for the price to be high as possible.

Attaching a value to the business

Information requirements

There is a vast amount of information that you must acquire about the business, its management, production and other systems, clients and competition to assist you in determining a price you will be prepared to pay. Make sure that you have all this information at your disposal for the assessments you have to make. This is a very technical area and I will try to simplify it for the purposes of our discussion, but certainly consult business experts when you want to finalise your decision to buy. Here I will only provide you with guidance on simple assessments.

Your primary objective here is to attach a price to the business: that price that will make financial sense to you. You do not want to overpay on the purchase of the business, because it will take a long time to recover the money paid to give you a good return on your investment. That will be throwing away good money. You want to drive this price as far down as you possibly can. Before you begin, make sure that you do the following to gather the information you need to have about the business:

- Obtain registration documents demonstrating that the seller is the owner of the business and can enter into a binding agreement to sell. If not, you will need signed resolutions by the owner(s) mandating the seller to dispose of their business. You do not want to deal with the wrong person.
- Obtain the balance sheet, i.e. a statement of financial position or statement of assets and liabilities, as discussed above, in order to identify assets and liabilities.
- Obtain an income statement, i.e. a statement of performance or trading or a profit-and-loss statement, as discussed above, for the most recent years in which the seller has owned and managed the business.
- Obtain a list of assets, such as plant, fixtures and fittings, equipment and computers, which the seller will be selling. These must be provided in support of the balance sheet, but you will need to obtain the most recent valuations of these assets. Generally they will be shown on the balance sheet at the prices the owner paid for them when they were acquired less any losses in value (depreciation) that the owner anticipates they have sustained. This is often not the market value of these assets if they were to be disposed of in an open market.
- Obtain an independent certification confirming that the financial statements presented to you by the seller are accurate. You need to guard against the risk of being misled into believing that what you are buying has huge potential, only to discover the opposite when it is too late.
- Obtain some proof that the assets referred to above are indeed owned by the seller. Title deeds, logbooks and signed representations by the owner will be necessary.
- Obtain copies of all contracts that the business has entered into, e.g. leases for premises, rentals of equipment, contracts with labour, etc. that you may have to carry out when the purchase goes through.

- Obtain details of any stock that the owner wishes to sell and how the stock will be counted and valued at settlement.
- Establish that any plant and equipment is in good working order. You may need to consult a qualified tradesperson. Have motor vehicles and machinery mechanically inspected. Do not assume that equipment is in good condition, as it can be very costly if you have to make major repairs or, even worse, replace an essential piece of equipment.

Use of experts

Working with the information that you will have in hand will not be easy, and requires highly skilled individuals in various fields. Make sure that you contact such experts for advice and guidance.

- A licensed **business valuer** will be able to advise you on the current market value of the business you are considering buying. We will look more closely at how this works.
- Your **accountant** will be able to advise you on the vendor's financial statements, the market value of the business, tax issues, and appropriate business structure options, and to assist with the budgets, cash-flow forecasts, and projected financial statements for your feasibility study.
- Your **lawyer** can provide legal advice on both the lease for the business premises and the offer to purchase, and recommend appropriate conditions to be written into an offer, which, if not fulfilled, will enable you to withdraw your offer without any penalty.

Valuation methods

In the section that follows I will merely introduce in very basic terms the various valuation methods that you can apply in given circumstances. Clearly, I do not expect you to be an expert in the field after reading this, but I trust that you will have a good idea of what the experts look at when they attach values to businesses.

There are three methods of valuing businesses, each of which can be the most suitable in specific circumstances. These are:

1. book value;
2. multiple earnings; and
3. discounted cash flows.

Book value

The book value of a business is, in essence, its worth at values that are presented in the balance sheet at the time of sale. With this method, you simply attach prices to the assets and liabilities of the business and pay the net difference. In the example shown in the section on the balance sheet above, the business has assets of R740 000 and liabilities of R620 000 and is therefore worth the retained earnings of R120 000 in its books. In theory, paying anything above R120 000 for this business would be paying a premium, which you do not want to do. Conversely, acquiring this business at a price below this would be getting it at a discount, which is desirable. Your negotiating point is the worth of this business, namely R120 000.

This valuation method is called the book value, which means the value in the book. The question is, who writes "the book"? In reality, the book is written by the very management and owners of the company that want to sell. So, in fact, you run a risk of buying assets that are overvalued and liabilities that are undervalued. The minute you enter the business after the purchase, the chairs and computers could start breaking down, or the vehicles pile up in maintenance, and you try to sell them, only to realise that you cannot even realise a fraction of what you paid to acquire them!

This means that you should never trust sellers with respect to the values of the assets and liabilities of the business they are selling. Engage experts in the field. There are industry experts on motor vehicles who will attach true and independent values to the vehicles you are buying with the business, property experts who will tell you whether the business premises are fairly valued, and so on. When all is done, you will come up with a restated balance sheet for the business that reflects the values that you are comfortable with and at which you are prepared to buy the business.

Finally, make sure that there are schedules of these assets and liabilities that you are purchasing and get the seller to sign off on them. You do not want to be surprised by people coming in to claim what they say are their assets, but which you have already paid for. In most cases you should be able to change the legal titles of the assets (e.g. bond registrations, logbooks, etc.) to make sure that the ownership of the assets reverts to you at the point of transfer of the business. In other cases, the seller should certify in writing that the assets belong to her and that no other, external parties have any claim to them.

Multiple earnings

This is a much more complex technique of valuing a business. I will try to simplify it, at a risk of oversimplifying it and being in trouble with my colleagues in the field. The basis for this method is that you accept that what you are buying is the *future potential* of the business to make money. With the previous method, you were buying the *past performance* of the business and the accumulated wealth that the business has been generating. With this technique, you are in fact buying its potential to generate wealth.

The method focuses on the income statement, which is the statement of the performance of the business, rather than the balance sheet as advocated in the book value method. If we work with the example above, you will notice that the business generated a net profit of R95 000. Of course this was before income tax, as we will discuss in the following chapters. This number is called EBIT (earnings before interest and tax). The value of the business will be based on these earnings.

Now, to attach the value, you need an understanding of how many years it should take for the business to pay for itself. There are statistical and industry data available that will give you these indications. To give a simple example, it is common knowledge that most assets, like vehicles, have a lifespan of five years. That is why they are mostly depreciated over five years and financed over five years. That means the *multiple* of earnings for such assets is 5. In simple terms, if you are to purchase an asset that will generate earnings of R10 000 for your business, that asset should not be purchased at over R50 000 (i.e. R10 000 x 5).

Let's go back to our business. We have noted that it has generated earnings of R95 000. The question is, to what extent were these earning abnormal, so that they will not recur in future years? Maybe the company had a very good year. In this regard you want to look at the trend of earnings and determine the average earnings before you apply a multiple. Your next step is to look at the industry multiples and apply those to the earnings. If in this case the industry multiple is 7, it means that the company is valued at R95 000 x 7 = R665 000.

Using a multiple is not as simple as picking up the industry multiple and applying it to the earnings of the company you want to buy to determine the price. Some factors need to be applied to the industry norm before you can confirm the multiple. For instance, if the management of the company will resign on purchase, if there are no standing contracts and if the location of the company is not in a prime area, those factors will have the effect of reducing the multiple and therefore the earnings. This is why you may need to engage the experts before you make a grave mistake by overvaluing the company and losing from day one.

Discounted cash flows

I do not want to dwell too much on this as it is to a large extent relevant to mergers and acquisitions of big companies. It is highly unlikely that you will find yourself as a small company compelled to use this method. It also carries with it some serious speculation and projections. Let's have a brief discussion, nevertheless.

The first step is to establish the projected cash flows of the entity you want to buy over a reasonable period, say five years or a period determined by industry experts. These projections will be based on cash receipts from customers and interest from banks and other investments, and cash payments to suppliers, labour and other overheads. In this regard you will have to rely a lot on what the existing owners and management are projecting, and apply your own risk factors to such projections. They are inclined to increase the value of receipts and reduce the payments to inflate the net future cash flows. Sellers are also prone to innocent aggressive speculations to your detriment. Have your experts around you when this exercise is performed.

Consider the following simple example:

	YEAR 1	YEAR 2	YEAR 3	YEAR 4	YEAR 5	TOTAL
Receipts	100 000	130 000	170 000	210 000	260 000	870 000
Payments	60 000	75 000	100 000	125 000	190 000	550 000
Net cash flows	40 000	55 000	70 000	85 000	70 000	320 000

If you study the table of cash flows above, you will realise that the value of this company is actually R320 000. That is the cash flow that it should generate over the speculated time. You cannot offer an amount above this, otherwise you will be losing over time. Conversely, an amount below this is your gain, assuming that the company performs to these projections.

The next thing to realise is that these cash flows are in the future, and typically in an inflationary environment the value of money drops over time. This implies that the R70 000 that you will generate in year 3 is worth less than that today, simply because of the time value of money. If you pay R320 000 for this business today, to realise R320 000 over five years, it stands to reason that you will lose on the deal. The seller will certainly score because he will realise his future value today and escape inflation.

This then means that you must find a mechanism to discount these future projected cash flows by a factor that reflects the time value of money. That factor could be the average weighted cost of capital, or the cost of debt if you will be raising a loan to purchase this business, or simply the projected inflation factor. Once again, you need to be guided by the experts. For the purposes of this exercise, let us assume that the said factor is 10%. You then have to discount the cash flows by this factor as depicted in the table on the next page.

	YEAR 1	YEAR 2	YEAR 3	YEAR 4	YEAR 5	TOTAL
Receipts	100 000	130 000	170 000	210 000	260 000	870 000
Payments	60 000	75 000	100 000	125 000	190 000	550 000
Net cash flows	40 000	55 000	70 000	85 000	70 000	320 000
Discounted cash flows	36 360	45 450	52 590	58 060	43 460	235 930

The discounted value of the business is now R235 930, significantly lower than the R320 000 we had previously calculated. It is now much more realistic and would not expose you to financial losses if the projections did indeed materialise.

A few words of advice

The values that have been calculated, whether on the book value, multiple earnings or discounted cash-flows, are the *break-even values* of the business. This means that if they are accurate, you are neither gaining nor losing by purchasing the business. They are your starting point in the negotiations. In order to gain, you need to negotiate below these values.

Remember that you are buying because you believe you can enhance the value of this business by your presence in it. If you are not going to do anything differently, maybe there is little point in buying at these values, as you are not making any impact.

Consider retaining key management in the business and putting that into the negotiations. Their departure might prove detrimental to the future of your business. They are familiar with the ins and outs of the business, have relationships with the customers and know the tricks of the trade. Do not be carried away by emotions and a quest for power. In the long run, you may lose badly.

CHAPTER 8

Drawing up a business plan

- What is a business plan?
- How does it help me?
- How do I do it?
- When must I do it?
- Who can help me with drawing up a business plan?

What is a business plan?

In the previous chapter we discussed the various financial structures available for your business to start and grow. There is truly a plethora of institutions that can provide financial assistance for your venture. The downside of these institutions is that they will not just fund any business as soon as they receive a request. They are extremely formal in their approach and will conduct an in-depth analysis before they can release the funds to your venture.

A primary assessment that they will want to make is, *Can the business make sufficient money to give us the required return on our investment?* If the potential investors are in government or in state-owned entities, there are a few more fundamental questions that they will seek to answer, such as:

- Will the business provide employment opportunities?
- Will the business assist in alleviating poverty?

- Will the business help to bridge the gap between the first and second economies?
- Will the business develop and provide infrastructure?

No investor can immediately pick up this information if you simply say you want to open a hairdressing salon and you need a loan of R75 000. Surely they will need much more from you.

A business plan provides that kind of insight. It is a fallacy to think that a business plan is helpful only to the investor. A well-researched and well-crafted business plan is helpful primarily to you, the entrepreneur! It tells you exactly whether you are gambling with money or entering into a viable venture. It is easy to fall into the trap of massaging the business plans to appease the funders, mostly at our own expense. Remember, they will give you a loan, but you will have to pay it back, with interest. If the concept does not seem to provide *you* with security that you are not throwing yourself into hell, abandon it and venture into something else. You yourself should be convinced that it will work before you try to convince the financing institution.

If you are convinced that the business concept and its dynamics make sense, then you can package it for the investor. We need to tap into the mind of an investor and try to ascertain what they might require before they can release the funds. The six sections of a winning business plan are discussed later in this chapter. Make sure that you cover all these sections thoroughly before you release your business plan to a potential funder.

Funders are thorough in their assessments. They will not risk their funds on a concept that will not work. They will ask uncomfortable questions. They will want proof of the claims that you make in the plan, verify your assessments and apply their risk factors to your potentially overly optimistic utterances. They will do their own research and perform a due diligence on your venture to assess its potential. Investors are very risk averse, and they do their homework!

Uses of a business plan

What is a business plan, and what is it useful for? This is a question we all have. Many of us think a business plan is merely a document that you submit to the bank when you need finance. The following people will want to read your business plan at some point in the life of your business:

1. The financier. We will talk extensively about the use of the business plan to the financier, as it is the crux of this chapter.
2. The potential investor or business partner. It is critical that your business plan should be as up to date as possible so that you can show it to, and discuss it with, potential investors and other people who may have an interest in your business and wish to finance your growth.
3. Yourself. You will always need to improve your operations, enhance your negotiating capacity and generate growth. A business plan will give you the direction that your business is taking and the steps that you intend taking to drive the business forward.

Putting a business plan together

Drawing up a business plan is an extremely tedious exercise. It requires that you have all your wits about you. As I will demonstrate, it contains a mixture of highly technical and non-technical information and needs to be packaged in a manner that will be not only logical to the reader but also appealing. I have two bits of advice here:

1. Before you draft your plan, read up on the specific requirements of the financier you want to approach. Financiers have explicit requirements and you want to ensure that your plan covers those requirements.
2. Consult with the experts in crafting business plans. They have dealt with the financiers and are very aware of what to look out for as they craft your plan.

I have also developed a *Business Plan Generator* that will help you develop your own draft business plan in the comfort of your home. This is a very user-friendly step-by-step guide to the development of a business plan. It probes you on the questions that the funders will ask you and makes you think about the elements of your business in order to satisfy both you and the potential investor in your business. For information on how you can obtain this tool, visit my website at www.tzulu.co.za.

Try to refrain from getting other people to do the business plan for you. It is, after all, your business and your plan, and you should own it! Engage professionals only for advice and guidance, and also for help with the appropriate language that you might not be very familiar with. Good assessors of these plans will call the owners and management around the table for an interview. They will do this to satisfy themselves that *you*, and not only the contracted compiler of the business plan, know what you are talking about and are familiar with the dynamics of the business you are entering into. From their perspective, there is no point in financing the venture on the basis of a document compiled by someone else and hoping to recover their investment from you, when you were not party to the developed plan that they relied on and scrutinised when assessing whether to grant you finance.

Basic elements of a business plan

Before I get into the technical configuration of the plan, these are the basic requirements that your plan should meet:

Business information

Make sure that you introduce the business to the potential funder at the start of your document. The following information is critical:

- name of the entity;
- form of ownership (sole proprietor, partnership, close corporation or company;

- registration documents;
- correspondence details (telephone numbers, addresses, email details, etc.);
- names and identity numbers of the owners; and
- line of business (industry in which the business operates).

There is also no harm in presenting the names of the bankers, lawyers and accountants. It gives credibility to the profile of the business.

Executive summary

You must never forget that the people who read and interact with your business plan have hundreds and thousands of other business plans to go through; their time is limited. They can get very impatient if they read rambling stories and cannot get a clear idea of where they are going. Contrary to the common approach, particularly in the African culture, of giving background information first before you make a request, *an effective approach to the business plan is to make a request first, before you tell too many stories.*

In this way you allow the financier to dissect your request quickly and take a decision on whether to proceed and the direction to take. Does your request for finance go to the Business Development Section, or does it go to the Loan Department, or does it get sent to the Properties Division of the bank? Is it going to be mainstream finance, or will it be looked at by the SMME (small, medium and micro enterprises) section of the financing institution? It is imperative that the plan gives that kind of direction to the reader succinctly. The following are key ingredients of the executive summary:

- nature of finance required (loan, equity or grant);
- amount required;
- purpose of the finance (vehicle, property or working capital finance);
- period of finance;
- key ratios and numbers (net income projections, balance sheet projections, cash-flow projections, returns on investments, dividend projections, etc.);

- for an existing business, key historic ratios (net annual income, current balance sheet and cash flows, current average returns on investments, dividend trends, etc.); and
- employment opportunities that come with the investment.

There may be more that will come into the executive summary than what is captured here. The point is, you want to whet the appetite of the investors sufficiently for them to want to read through the proposal without spending a lot of their time. You want them to read through the rest of the document with insight and knowing the questions they would be seeking answers to before they can support your venture with a financial injection. You are making their work easier by providing an effective executive summary, and in that you will certainly improve the view they have of you and of your business.

Detail of the business plan

Now you can come to the detail of the business plan and discuss extensively the dynamics of your venture, the reasons for your application and the ability of the business to service the loan or finance required. If you have done the conceptualisation of your business as discussed in Chapter 4, this should be a walk in the park. The thought process is similar, although the packaging might be somewhat different.

In the following diagram I have put together the six sections of a business plan for your consideration. Each of these sections will be discussed in turn.

1. BUSINESS CONCEPT		2. MARKET
• Describe the industry • Describe the sector clearly		• Does the market exist? • Where is the market identified? • What is the size and your share? • How will the market be penetrated?

4. BUSINESS STRATEGY		3. PRODUCT/SERVICE
• How is production going to be structured? • How will the value chain be tackled? • How are critical success factors going to be managed?		• Description of product/service • How is it produced/delivered? • Advantages over existing products • Intellectual property of the product

5. LEADERSHIP & MANAGEMENT		6. FINANCES
• Assumptions • Projections • Requirements • Sensitivity analysis		• Who are the key personnel? • Experience and qualifications

1. The business concept

In this section you need to introduce the concept of your business and the dynamics of the industry. For instance, the concept of one of the businesses I manage is information management in an industry that keeps information in hard-copy documents. Therefore, the concept is primarily document management or archiving, and secondarily scanning documents and managing the process flows of information to increase ease of access and security. Your concept might be provision of rented transportation or provision of security to private and business properties. Describe your concept explicitly so that the reader can know what your business is about.

Discuss why you have chosen such a concept and the trends in the industry that would indicate support for your concept. In the case of my information management example, I would discuss the fact that information is the central nervous system of a business and a legislated requirement. I would explain that documents take up space, which is at a premium nowadays. I would go on to say that information management requires investment in systems and infrastructure that come at exorbitant costs. I would then say that because this activity is not the core of a business but simply a necessary evil, most businesses are prepared to outsource it, citing examples, and illustrating the advent of my concept.

You must even go a step further and give details of the budget that customers have put aside for the services you will be offering. Industry journals and publications can assist you with such statistics. What you are attempting to achieve here is to illustrate that the concept has a buyer and is worth entering into.

In this section you also have to discuss the social impact of your business in detail. How many people do you anticipate employing? How many are currently in your employ and what are the demographics? What are other social issues on which your business has an impact? Where is your business located, and why is it located there? Could this be a value-chain issue, or merely one of proximity to the target market? All these details are critical for a reader to understand the business and the sector dynamics around your business.

2. The market

In this section you want to demonstrate, not with emotion but with facts and figures, that there is a market for what you will be offering. It could be a new product or service altogether, where you have a tough battle to demonstrate that it will be bought. Discuss the market trends with regard to your product as well as the market sentiments about the existing products over which yours will have the upper hand.

There are two critical questions to answer in this regard:

1. Is there a market?
2. How big do you anticipate your share of the market to be?

These are by no means easy questions to answer, and they require much from you before you can provide details in the business plan. In a perfect world you would have engaged market research specialists to conduct market studies and answer question 1 in a much more scientific way. Certainly, if you are engaging in a huge project that requires substantial amounts of money to finance, it is worth making an investment in market research in order to be sure and to convince the funder that the market does exist. Smaller investments do not warrant this exercise. You might just contact a couple of potential buyers to make representations on your behalf to indicate that they will be interested in your product and in supporting you once your business is up and running.

Market segmentation

The issue is: what is the segment of the market into which you will be launching your product? This needs to be defined thoroughly for the evaluator of the proposal. It has to be a segment that is probably untapped or most likely to respond positively to your company and your product. Again you need to discuss in detail what that segment is and why you have decided to launch into and service that particular segment. The segment you target could be SMMEs, as in my case where I intend to gain that segment with this book; it could be large corporates because of the BEE mileage that they want to gain on their scorecard by supporting your business, or it could be the public sector because that is where the greatest need for your product exists.

What is your marketing strategy?

A typical investor will want to know how you are going to penetrate the market. Business is aggressively competitive, and established role players are very quick to reject a newcomer. They will come up with all sorts of tricks to make sure that your business does not survive. They will reduce their prices ridiculously, launch marketing campaigns that you cannot afford to compete with and have serious promotions of their products. The question is, How are you going to react to these strategies? What will your strategy be? Remember, you are a relatively unknown player and the nature of people is to approach and buy from the "tried and tested". What is going to be your competitive advantage?

What is your distribution strategy?

This is another important issue to consider and discuss. How will your products be distributed to the market? What channels will you use, and why are you planning to distribute your products in that way? Distribution can either be directly to the final consumer through physical means where orders are placed over the phone or via the internet (as is increasingly the case nowadays), or it could be by setting up an outlet or outlets and having customers knock on your door to purchase. It could also be done through a network of retailers or distributors where your product is, in theory, sold to them and they then sell it to the eventual customers. You could have contracts with, for instance, Pick n Pay, where they will form a distribution or retail channel for your products.

It is critical to pin this down in detail as it will have a major bearing on your cost structure. Direct distribution carries substantial transportation costs, whereas setting up an outlet will have costs associated with stock holding and infrastructure management. This analysis must tie in with the financial analysis of your company.

3. The product/service

You might argue that discussing your product or service is necessary even before you engage in the market discussion, as it enables the reader to understand the product/service and place it in the market. Honestly, I do not think it matters. This section of your plan articulates exactly what the product or service is. You will recall that we elaborated on the importance of this in the chapter on business modelling. The crucial point here is to make the reader understand precisely what you will be selling. You cannot say you are entering into consulting, because it is such a vast terrain, with different fields of consulting requiring different skills sets. Similarly, you cannot say you are in IT, because this too is rather vague. Will you be selling hardware, software, networking, programming, or all of the above? If you are going to be programming, I would expect to see programmers in your business, which will not be an expectation if you are going to be distributing computers and printers. As I have said before, we tend to draw up these vague business plans that create a lot of questions in the minds of the evaluators.

You also must discuss the legal issues around the product in detail. Can someone else enter the market with the same or a similar product, or do you have intellectual property rights over the product? Are you the sole distributor of that product, or is it distributed in the open market? These factors could have serious implications for the viability of your concept and would make potential investors either excited or unenthusiastic about your product.

Do not be modest, but remain truthful about the uniqueness of your product when compared to competitor products. If it offers unique benefits, state them. If it performs multiple functions and incorporates a number of products in one, say so. These are the unique selling points (USPs) of your product that will make it more beneficial to the market and attractive to funders. For instance, there are many books about running a business available in the market, but few are South African and even fewer condense the issues of business from a risk perspective, as this one does. This gives the book a quality of uniqueness that hopefully will make you, the reader, feel attracted to it.

4. The business strategy

This is the section where you need to dissect your business. Here you are explaining *how* you are planning to do things. You are visualising the business in operation and writing down all the critical issues with regard to its operation.

Production

Describe the production process. What ingredients and what quantities go into the final product? What is the production cycle, and how long will it take to effect production? The business production process normally has the following components:

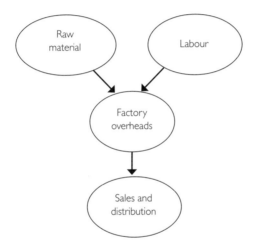

The raw material component of the business must be described. What kinds of material the production cycle requires, in what quantities, and where they will be sourced from, are important matters to mention. The prices of the material must also be factored into the financial analysis. If you are in a retail or service environment, you obviously have it easy in this regard as your business does not involve raw materials.

The labour component assists the financier to understand the cost of labour in the production process. How many workers are going to be employed, and where in the production process will they be located? How many will operate the machinery? How many will package? How many will be in stores responding to the production needs for material, and how many will be in quality control, distribution, transportation, etc? These are all issues to be ironed out in your plan.

The factory overheads are a necessary ingredient of a production operation. The plan should address overheads such as water, lights, costs of maintenance of the factory plant and machinery. Overheads cause costs to pile up and reduce profitability. These assessments must be made.

Thus far you have isolated and discussed all the ingredients that drive the costs of production of the final product. In a service environment it could be just labour costs at this stage. For retail operations you probably have to deal with costs of goods to be sold and the labour component. Now you need to discuss the distribution, sales and marketing processes to get the product to the final consumer. These also attract costs and must be understood by the financier. How are you going to distribute the product, and how much are the channels going to cost?

Administration

The business strategy must articulate how the overall business will be administered. This adds further labour costs and other costs such as communication, and information technology. A typical financier will want to assess whether you are not too heavy on administration and can drive certain costs down to make your model affordable. Remember, this is where people tend to provide for huge salaries and luxuries, which the business does not require in its infancy.

Machinery

You need to describe the nature and number of machines that your production process requires. The extent of investment in these machines needs to be quantified. Once again, this will have a bearing on the costs.

Risk management

As we discussed in the chapter on risk management, you need to identify significant business risks and describe how they will be managed.

5. Leadership and management

A significant area of focus when such plans are adjudicated is who is behind the business. A model may look great on paper but prove to be a flop in reality because the leadership do not have a clue of what they are doing. Alternatively, the model may start off on a bad footing and yet thrive because the leaders know how to react to crises and are experienced in the industry. This is what investors in your business want to know. They will not play a hands-on role in your business, and want to rely on the leadership and management to run and make a success of the company they are financing. You need to make sure that you sell the team that you have assembled adequately to the funders of your business.

Typically, the funders will look for the following:

- names and contact information of the leadership;
- demographic profile, such as age, experience, etc; and
- the roles they will be playing in the business.

Depending on the funders, information about the financial status of the leaders might be a requirement. Information on past and present engagements, judgements, defaults and so on could be required to assess the risk of funding an entity with leaders and managers of that calibre.

6. The finances

The final step, but arguably the most critical, is the packaging of the business plan into a financial model. Here you are demonstrating that the business will be profitable, and assuring the potential investor that her investment will be safe and the business will be able to repay the loan, or utilise the grant in the best interest of the funder, or yield the anticipated return on investment for the equity financier.

In this regard you need to package this demonstration very thoroughly to allow for such analysis. See www.tzulu.co.za for a software package that will assist you with this. It will put things into perspective and work out this analysis for you easily. The only issue, though, is that you will need to make sure you capture the costs completely and do not leave out costs that the program cannot guess as they are unique to your business.

Most funders would want you to make projections for a minimum of two years. Be very careful not to be unrealistically aggressive or optimistic in your estimates. Rather be honest upfront about the fact that the business will be slow than lead your business into a contract that you will not be able to honour.

The sensitivity of your estimates must also be presented to the funder. For instance, how sensitive is the market to price, and if you increase prices, to what extent will you lose volumes? How sensitive are your production costs to interest rate hikes and exchange rates, and how will your profitability be affected if these become unfavourable? You may want to present most-likely-case, worst-case and best-case scenarios for the financier, depending on their specific requirements. Regardless of the financier, however, you need to do this analysis for yourself.

A final word on the business plan

- Try to remain truthful in how you package all of this information in your plan. Lies or misrepresentations will come back to haunt you, and you will lose credibility with the financier.
- Even if you have engaged someone else to write the plan for you, own it. It is *your* plan and you will need to execute it in the way that you promised the financier.
- Read your plan over and over and make sure that you are comfortable with its contents. You may be asked to come for an interview to articulate it in person. You do not want to be found wanting.
- Test various scenarios until you come up with the best approach to your business and are convinced that it will make money even in the worst of times.
- Accumulate the costs as completely as possible and try to anticipate all costs. If in doubt, rather go with a pessimistic approach and be safe.
- Take pride in your plan. It shows when you are being interviewed.

CHAPTER 9

Drawing up a budget

- What is a budget?
- How does it help me?
- How do I do it?
- When must I do it?
- Who can help me with drawing up a budget?

I have come across a number of organisations that carry on their business without a budget. Many put a budget together at the point of preparing a business plan, but then never refer to that budget again and wonder why the business is not performing to their satisfaction. In this chapter I hope to demonstrate the importance of drawing up a budget, the mechanisms of keeping in touch with the budget, and the actual art of presenting a budget. We will also discuss the management accounts and what your business needs to keep tabs on, including control of the operations.

What is a budget?

As many would contend, a budget is a plan translated into figures, including finances. It articulates how you intend operating in a specified future period. In a way, we always prepare budgets, even in our private lives. Maybe we do not formalise it and put it on paper. But you know what you will do with the salary you earn. You know how much money you intend paying for your wedding to be successful. You even know what you will be spending your money on for your next trip. You have put together a plan of expenditure for Christmas against the bonus you will earn at work. These are all examples of a budget.

Nothing changes when it comes to a business. Maybe a budget for a business is much more complex than your personal budget. This I will unpack shortly, but the principles are exactly the same.

What if there is no budget?

Well, I think you can probably answer this question yourself. If there is no budget, it means that there is no plan or that the plan has not been translated into its financial implications. You are, in essence, launching your business blindly, and you will certainly run into problems. Let's consider a simple example.

Suppose you have a large sum of money and decide to build a house without a budget for the following:

- architectural designs,
- labour,
- building material,
- finishes, and
- paving.

Do you know what is likely to happen? You will buy tiles based on your liking for them instead of taking financial considerations into account, get very expensive finishes because they will look nice in your house, pay expensively for labour because the contractor looks reliable, and so on. And when the house needs roof trusses, there is no money left for them. When it is time to buy windows, you suddenly realise that you forgot about them; they just slipped your mind. The end result will be an unfinished house with a lot of expensive material sitting in boxes. This is because the finances and the material items were not adequately managed.

With a budget, you have better control over the funds. You put limits on the expenditure on certain items and control your taste. You know when some items have cost less than you anticipated and you can spend that money on your taste. Similarly, you know when some items have cost more than you thought, so you start moving funds around to make sure that you can acquire them. All of this is achievable if you have put a budget together – not when you are operating blindly.

Likewise, in business, the budget is a critical tool in managing material and finances. You need to make sure that the expenditure is prioritised and that you are spending money according to your plans.

How do you put a budget together?

Remember that a budget is a plan of expenditure. Like all expenditure plans, budgets are underpinned by income projections. This means that you need to follow an income base for the development of the budget. I want us to follow a step-by-step guide to budget preparation.

Step 1: Determine an income budget

You cannot budget to spend what you do not have. The first step is to establish what you have, or what you will have. Your income estimates will drive how much you will spend. The difficulty in business is that the income is never known. Unlike your salary, which is fixed and comes into your account every month, your business income is not so easy to ascertain. While some months are very good and you generate an income that exceeds your expectations, other months are disappointing and you can barely make ends meet.

There are two issues when it comes to determining income: how much you will make, and when sales will become cash. We need to realise that what will make our businesses work, by and large, is when the sales are converted into cash. Let me remain focused and deal with one issue at a time.

Income determination

There are two factors that affect your revenue or income in business. The one is volume and the other is price, as in the formula below:

VOLUME x PRICE = REVENUE

If I plan for my volume to be 100 units at a price of R10 per unit, my revenue budget is 100 x R10 = R1 000. If I sell more than one item, I need to perform this exercise for all the items that I will sell; in other words, for each item, I need to determine how many units I will sell and determine the price levels for each of the commodities. The calculation will follow the model presented below:

\multicolumn{4}{c}{MONTHLY REVENUE BUDGET}			
Item	Volume	Price per unit	Amount
Cellphones	300	R4 000	R1 200 000
Cell chargers	420	R80	R33 600
Cell batteries	80	R340	R27 200
Total			**R1 250 800**

This cellphone outlet that sells only three items (cellphones, batteries and chargers) anticipates that it will make R1 250 800 for the month. Obviously, this cannot just be a wish list, because our next steps will be to make a number of commitments based on this income budget. If it does not materialise, there will be major financial and operational disruptions to the business. We therefore cannot simply guess these numbers!

The volume budget depends on a number of factors, one being the price. If the price is right the volumes may be achieved, but if these prices are steep and not competitive, the volumes are at risk. Other factors will include the quality of our product, the location of our outlet, the marketing that has been done, and even the response from our competitors. It is a fairly intense exercise, but if we are to come up with a realistic income budget, we have to think about all these factors.

The price budget is also based on competitor analysis as well as, very importantly, the cost of the product. There is no point in buying cellphones from suppliers at a price of R4 250 and selling them at R4 000.

If this exercise were to be done thoroughly, you would have to draw up a budget for every single item that you have in stock and intend to sell. But you can just imagine how it would be for a supermarket such as Shoprite that sells many items. That is why you can make averages across similar products. For instance, these cellphones do not have to be identical in looks and price, but we can average it out and determine the average prices. What is also an advantage in the modern business world is that there are systems that maintain all stock items and generate reports of sales, stock holding and stock movements that assist us to determine these budgets.

My advice is to stay conservative with the income budget. The income budget is at a huge risk of not being achievable, and you need to factor that risk into your projections.

What we have just done is a monthly revenue budget. We need such a revenue budget for a period of at least one year. It stands to reason that the months in a year are not all the same. Some months are quiet and people focus on other things; buying cellphones is not on their list of priorities. They are recovering from an extravagant festive season, for instance, and children have to be sent to school. During periods such as the festive season, however, people have received bonuses and want to spoil themselves, and you will make more money. The annual revenue budget will resemble the table on page 118.

In our example, we have assumed that there will be no price increases throughout the year, which, of course, is probably unreasonable. If you know that you will be increasing the prices, obviously the revenue will increase from that point on, thus generating higher revenues by the end of the year. Remember, this revenue is exclusive of VAT. The VAT does not belong to you but to SARS, and should not be counted as your revenue.

Timing of revenue
Earlier I alluded to the fact that revenue is not cash, particularly to a business that sells on credit or that delivers before it gets paid. Most companies that contract with government will tell you that the processes take a very long time and payments do not get effected when you require the funds.

ANNUAL REVENUE BUDGET

Item	Price per unit	Jan	Feb	Mar	Apr	May	Jun	Jul	Aug	Sep	Oct	Nov	Dec	Total Volume	Amount
Cell-phones	R4 000	240	270	300	300	300	300	200	300	300	300	300	400	3 510	R14 040 000
Cell chargers	R80	320	390	420	420	420	420	300	420	420	420	420	450	4 820	R385 600
Cell batteries	R340	60	70	80	80	80	80	50	80	80	80	80	100	920	R312 800
							Total								R14 738 400

118 DRAWING UP A BUDGET

It is important to keep this in mind, as it has a major bearing on the cash flows of your business. Also make provision for non-payment of some of the amounts you will have invoiced. These are the realities of business.

Step 2: Determine a capital expenditure budget

Now that you know how much revenue you will generate, and have factored in all forms of unexpected negative eventualities, you can draw up a plan of how the money will be spent. Even here, I need to point out upfront that these plans must not put you at risk, and the timing of expenses must not be too close to your revenue streams. Remember that most, if not all, expenditure legally binds you to certain third parties. You do not want to over-commit yourself and your business, nor do you want to live by running away from creditors.

I want us to deal with the capital expenditure budget first and then focus on the operational expenditure budget. Capital expenditure is by nature the kind of expenditure that brings assets to the business. The purchase of vehicles, expansion of the factory plant, and the purchase of computers, equipment and furniture would constitute such expenditure. These are items that you would not purchase year on year.

It is highly likely that these would have been purchased from a loan at the time you were starting up your business and you would not have to fund them yourself, but remember that they wear out and need to be replaced at some point. Further, if your business is doing very well, you may need to expand and buy more of these assets. Your strategy for growth and expansion will answer that question. If there is a need to acquire such assets, you need to factor that into your budget and reserve funds for them accordingly.

You need to determine the strategy for acquiring these assets. There are three basic ways in which you can finance the acquisition of capital items:

1. You may want to pay cash for them, in which case you need to have this in the capital expenditure budget.
2. You may want to finance their acquisition, in which case they still get into the capital expenditure budget, but you reflect a loan in your cash flows to show that these assets will not be funded from your operating revenues.

3. You may want to rent these assets instead of owning them. There are many companies that offer packages where you lease assets and pay on a month-by-month basis. In these cases your rental payments will actually be included in your operational expenditure budget and not in the capital expenditure budget that we are discussing at present.

How you finance the acquisition of assets depends on your cash flows and the financial stability of your business. It may also depend on the asset in question. If you do not need the asset in your ordinary business activities and only require it for a project, it is best to lease it, as investing in it will not yield future benefits for your entity. If, however, the asset is integral to your business, it is advisable to purchase it. Whether this is done through a loan or from your cash flows would depend on the available cash, your other future financial commitments and your ability to raise loan funding.

Now you have determined your capital expenditure budget, which may be a simple table like the one below. This simply sets out the nature of assets that you intend acquiring, the date on which such acquisitions will be made and the amount to be invested. I have assumed for illustration that the investments will be from your cash flows. In other words, you will not lease or finance the acquisitions from loan finance. You are confident that the cash to be generated from sales will be adequate to cover such acquisitions. This is obviously very desirable for any business as you are not indebted to anyone and have ownership of the assets you keep in your business. This, as I have mentioned before, is not always the most practical method of acquiring assets.

Always remember that capital expenditure does not go to the "bottom line". I do not want to get too technical at this stage, but your investment in assets will not affect your profitability. Remember that such assets are to be used over a lengthy period of time, therefore they are investments. You do not lose money immediately when you purchase a car, as you can always sell it and recover some money. It therefore cannot go into your books as an expense but as an investment of some sort. The truth is that it loses value over time and it is only the value lost that you will recognise as an expense, not the price you paid to acquire it.

ANNUAL CAPITAL BUDGET

Item	Jan	Feb	Mar	Apr	May	Jun	Jul	Aug	Sep	Oct	Nov	Dec	Amount
Bakkie		230 000											230 000
Office furniture	50 000					100 000							150 000
Warehouse furniture											1 500 000		1 500 000
Warehouse equipment												340 000	340 000
						Total							**R2 220 000**

You will recall from the revenue budget that we anticipated that we will generate revenue of R14 738 400 during the year. Now we are budgeting to spend R2 220 000 of this revenue on purchasing assets. We are left, therefore, with R12 518 400 for operational expenditure and our profits.

The next question, before we go into the operational expenditure budget, is whether there will be money on hand to acquire these assets we plan to purchase. In other words, will we have R50 000 to purchase equipment in January, R230 000 for a bakkie in February, etc.? You will recall that in the income or revenue budget we discussed the timing of revenue. This is where this exercise comes in handy, as it will indicate to us whether there will be cash in the account of the business to discharge these capital commitments. Well, looking at the rate of sales of around a million a month in this case and considering that these sales are to the retail market, which pays cash on delivery of these items, it does not appear likely that we will have a problem purchasing these assets.

Step 3: Determine an operational expenditure budget

In this phase of the budget preparation process, you want to establish how much you will spend on operations. This exercise is necessary to determine whether the operations are not too expensive and you need to limit some expenses. You need to think very carefully about the operational requirements of your business. Once again, at this stage you would have gone quite far with this thinking because you would have conceptualised your business and developed a model as we discussed earlier in this book. All you are doing now is to anticipate the costs to make your model work in order to test its financial viability and ensure that it succeeds.

Let's get straight to it. The table on the next page will help you with the structure of your operational expenditure budget. This should not be a "thumb-suck" exercise, and you need to be as practical as possible when you determine your operational expenditure budget. This can make or break your business. You will need to commit to this expenditure once you have finalised this exercise. You will recruit staff, apply for connections with Telkom and place orders for stock. If these costs exceed those in your budget it means that you have to go back to the drawing board, particularly if your

ANNUAL OPERATIONAL EXPENDITURE BUDGET

Item	Jan	Feb	Mar	Apr	May	Jun	Jul	Aug	Sep	Oct	Nov	Dec	Amount
Cost of sales	504 800	569 600	632 800	632 800	632 800	632 800	422 000	632 800	632 800	632 800	632 800	838 000	7 396 800
Cellphones	480 000	540 000	600 000	600 000	600 000	600 000	400 000	600 000	600 000	600 000	600 000	800 000	7 020 000
Cell chargers	12 800	15 600	16 800	16 800	16 800	16 800	12 000	16 800	16 800	16 800	16 800	18 000	192 800
Cell batteries	12 000	14 000	16 000	16 000	16 000	16 000	10 000	16 000	16 000	16 000	16 000	20 000	184 000
Salaries	60 000	60 000	60 000	60 000	60 000	60 000	65 000	65 000	65 000	65 000	65 000	65 000	750 000
Warehouse rent	15 000	15 000	15 000	15 000	15 000	15 000	15 000	15 000	15 000	15 000	15 000		165 000
Water and lights	1 300	1 300	1 300	1 300	1 300	1 300	1 300	1 300	1 300	1 300	1 300	1 300	15 600
Printing/stationery	3 000	3 000	3 000	3 000	3 000	3 000	3 000	3 000	3 000	3 000	3 000	3 000	36 000
Marketing	5 000	5 000	5 000	5 000	5 000	5 000	5 000	5 000	5 000	5 000	5 000	5 000	60 000
Telephone/fax	2 400	2 400	2 400	2 400	2 400	2 400	2 400	2 400	2 400	2 400	2 400	2 400	28 800
Travelling	10 000	10 000	2 200	2 200	2 200	2 200	2 200	2 200	2 200	2 200	2 200	2 200	42 000
TOTAL													**8 494 200**

revenue streams are too tight because, remember, it is your revenue that will fund these costs.

Some costs will reduce or increase depending on your business strategy for growth. You will notice in our example that the costs of travelling went down substantially after we bought our own bakkie in February. Practically, though, this gets negated by the depreciation of the bakkie, which we have not factored into our example. Again, our rental costs disappear after November because we have purchased our own warehouse.

Step 4: Put it together and review

Now that we have done all the budgets, we have to put all of this together and review it. The questions we are now asking are:

1. What is the anticipated level of performance of our business, and are we happy with it?
2. Are the revenues sufficient to cover our operational costs?
3. Can we finance our capital expenditure after we have financed our operations?
4. What is the sensitivity of revenue, and what risks are associated with revenue generation? Which costs can we do without?
5. What are the cash flows, and can we run on a month-to-month basis?

Any negative answers mean that we have to take another look at our cost structure. Maybe we are not ready to buy a warehouse, so we have to continue renting. Maybe we can make do with a smaller staff and reduce our payroll cost, etc. All of this will be determined from the affordability exercise.

The annual budget in the table below puts these things into perspective. If cellphone shops performed like this, I would have invested in one myself. You will notice that this business is sailing financially. Stock is obviously very easy to find at favourable prices. Gross profits are close to 50%. Basically we are doubling the price at which we bought the chargers. If our assessments of supply and the market are accurate, this line of business is what everyone would want to get into. Our operational costs are reasonably low, which helps us to drop a lot of our gross profits into the "bottom line".

ANNUAL OPERATIONAL EXPENDITURE BUDGET

Item	Jan	Feb	Mar	Apr	May	Jun	Jul	Aug	Sep	Oct	Nov	Dec	Amount
Sales	1 006 000	1 135 000	1 260 800	1 260 800	1 260 800	1 260 800	841 000	1 260 800	1 260 800	1 260 800	1 260 800	1 670 000	14 738 400
Cost of sales	504 800	569 600	632 800	632 800	632 800	632 800	422 000	632 800	632 800	632 800	632 800	838 000	7 396 800
Gross Profit	**501 200**	**565 400**	**628 000**	**628 000**	**628 000**	**628 000**	**419 000**	**628 000**	**628 000**	**628 000**	**628 000**	**832 000**	**7 341 600**
Salaries	60 000	60 000	60 000	60 000	60 000	60 000	65 000	65 000	65 000	65 000	65 000	65 000	750 000
Warehouse rent	15 000	15 000	15 000	15 000	15 000	15 000	15 000	15 000	15 000	15 000	15 000		165 000
Water/lights	1 300	1 300	1 300	1 300	1 300	1 300	1 300	1 300	1 300	1 300	1 300	1 300	15 600
Printing/stationery	3 000	3 000	3 000	3 000	3 000	3 000	3 000	3 000	3 000	3 000	3 000	3 000	36 000
Marketing	5 000	5 000	5 000	5 000	5 000	5 000	5 000	5 000	5 000	5 000	5 000	5 000	60 000
Telephone/fax	2 400	2 400	2 400	2 400	2 400	2 400	2 400	2 400	2 400	2 400	2 400	2 400	28 800
Travelling	10 000	10 000	2 200	2 200	2 200	2 200	2 200	2 200	2 200	2 200	2 200	2 200	42 000
Net Profit	**404 500**	**468 700**	**539 100**	**539 100**	**539 100**	**539 100**	**325 100**	**539 100**	**539 100**	**539 100**	**539 100**	**753 100**	**6 244 200**
Capital Expenditure	50 000	230 000				100 000					1 500 000	340 000	2 220 000
						NET PROFIT BEFORE TAX							4 024 200

DRAWING UP A BUDGET

We are more than able to finance our growth and purchase assets, and still make a killing! If only business were this great, but I hope you get the picture just in terms of the analysis you would need to do once you have consolidated your budget.

We certainly will pass this budget and want to go into business with it.

Management of the budget

What is left is to see this budget in practice. Things seldom go as planned in business. You will often make incorrect judgements, and reality will prove you wrong. This means that you must stay close to your plans and review them regularly to see if the real results contradict them, for better or worse. Expenses must be closely monitored. You need to get reports frequently that indicate to you whether things are going as planned. You do not want to sign that offer to purchase a warehouse if there will not be R1,5 million to pay for it. You will get into serious legal battles if you renege on such a transaction.

Every month you need to receive management accounts that will show you how your company has performed. Typically, these will show you the budget information and the actual results. They will then indicate how these vary and help you assess whether the variances make sense and how they can best be managed in the future. You want to get these reports as early as possible so that you can react in good time. The management accounts will look almost as presented in the table on the next page.

Over and above this information in the management accounts, you want to get monthly reports of the following:

1. debtors' age analysis, detailing the names of customers that owe you money and how long their debts have been outstanding, so that you can follow up on them;
2. creditors' age analysis, detailing the names of suppliers and creditors to whom you owe money and how long your debts have been outstanding;
3. inventory records and how well your inventory is moving, to determine whether you are adequately stocked; and

MANAGEMENT ACCOUNTS: JANUARY				
Item	Budget	Actual	Variance	Reason
Sales	1 006 000	950 000	56 000	Fewer sales than anticipated
Cost of sales	504 800	489 600	15 200	Lower costs due to fewer sales
Gross Profit	**501 200**	**460 400**	**40 800**	
Salaries	60 000	60 000	0	
Warehouse rent	15 000	14 950	50	Nominal amount
Water/lights	1 300	1 560	(260)	Increase in municipal rates
Printing/ stationery	3 000	2 100	900	Fewer invoices and envelopes utilised
Marketing	5 000	6 450	(1 450)	Additional cost of business cards, stamps
Telephone/fax	2 400	2 200	200	Fewer calls than anticipated
Travelling	10 000	9 500	500	Decrease in fuel price
Net Profit	**404 500**	**363 640**	**40 860**	
Capital Expenditure	**50 000**	**100 000**	**(50 000)**	Purchased all furniture at once to obtain discount

4. bank information and reconciliations to determine your future cash-flow decisions.

Not having this information is almost like running the business blindly. You will get surprises and be caught with "your pants down". Be proactive, and run your business like a business!

CHAPTER 10

Product costing

> - How do I determine the cost of my product?
> - How do I make sure that I do not sell at a loss?
> - How do I minimise the cost of my product?
> - How do I set price levels for my products?

The key to driving profitability in business is costing your products and services correctly. If we fail to do this, we expose our business to serious risks. A primary risk is to run our businesses at a loss. Remember that what customers respond to is the price, and once they accept that price, a contract has been concluded. Experts in contract law will tell you that when you mark your products on the shelf, you are in fact making an offer. When a customer picks up the product and goes with it to the till he or she is accepting the offer, which concludes a contract. You would place your business in extreme jeopardy if you turned around and said, "Oops, that price is not right, I must include another R5 for my electricity!" A customer would think you were out of your mind and might even abandon the purchase or refuse to pay the additional cost. Whether you won or lost the argument, you would have sent a message to potential customers that the prices marked on your commodities are fluid and may change at any time.

I have come across people who submitted proposals, especially for government tenders, where their pricing was just not correct because they could not anticipate correctly the costs involved in rendering that service.

Again, it becomes almost impossible to go back to the government client and say, "I would like to increase the prices I quoted you because that quote did not include transportation!" A client will rightfully tell you to get lost. In this chapter we shall deal with one issue: costing your products correctly! This will help you to price them right and make the long-awaited *profits*.

Make sure that you have your calculator in hand as we manoeuvre through this chapter, because there will be a lot of calculations to play with. It can get a bit confusing, but if you lock yourself away without disturbances, we should be fine.

Cost accumulation

Your business is going to be a never-ending machine that constantly makes you pay. Such payments will not even be on a consistent basis. For instance, you may be paying for the products as you purchase them, depending on whether you purchase them daily, every second day, and so on. You will pay your wages weekly, maybe monthly. Your transport costs will occur as and when you collect from or deliver to clients; your electricity and rentals will be paid monthly. Some costs may only occur once every five years, such as buying a van to collect your products, or tools to be used in the manufacturing process. In short, there will be a series of costs that you incur every day of your life. The basic rule is: find an effective way to classify and accumulate these costs so that you know exactly what you are paying for.

The question is: what are we accumulating these costs for? Ultimately you want to determine prices for your products, which you will mark on them for the customers will pay. You want to make sure that those prices will not result in your business running at a loss. Remember, you have one, and only one, avenue to recover your costs and make a profit – prices. If you leave out any of your costs when determining the price, you will pay that cost without recovering it from the customers. You can be sure that this will lead to serious losses. You want to accumulate costs so that you know how much it costs you to run your business. What you want to achieve is for this cost to be included in the price you set, so that the customer pays for it and you make a profit.

Let's look at a simple example of a retail outlet that sells just one item: reams of printing paper. Sure, there may not be such an outlet, but let's build this concept systematically so that we do not get confused. All we do for now in our shop is to buy reams of paper from a supplier, sell them to customers and make a profit. We have a small van that we use to transport these reams from the supplier. The reams are stored in a little warehouse with just two offices, one for the owner and the other for the administrator, who does invoicing and ordering and follows up on payments from the customers. We have decided to avoid selling on credit and want customers to come through the door to buy paper. We sell paper in reams, and do not want to open a ream and sell loose sheets of paper. A very simple business concept, but it works for us! We have customers buying from us every day.

The table below reflects our costs:

ITEM	COST	FREQUENCY
Transport – fuel (to collect stock)	R3 000	Monthly
Rent for the offices and warehouse	R7 500	Monthly
Water and lights	R 800	Monthly
Consumables	R 150	Monthly
Vehicles	R30 000	Once off
Racks	R2 000	Once off
Computers	R5 000	Once off
Salary – administrator	R6 000	Monthly
Maintenance – van	R 400	Monthly
Insurance – van	R 250	Monthly

Now we know how much it costs us to run our business. One difficulty is that the costs of running our operation are in varying intervals, some monthly and others once off. Our next challenge is to translate all costs to a uniform time measure. Costs such as vehicles we have to translate by asking ourselves how much of the vehicle we are using monthly if we buy it for R30 000. In other words, how long will it last in our business before it is scrapped? Here you will need to consult asset experts who can give you guidelines. Let us say the vehicle and the racks will last us five years and the computers only three years. Translating these costs into monthly checks will give us the following:

ITEM	COST	FREQUENCY
Transport – fuel (to collect stock)	R3 000	Monthly
Rent for the office and warehouse	R7 500	Monthly
Water and lights	R 800	Monthly
Consumables	R 150	Monthly
Vehicles (R30 000/60 months)	R 500	Monthly
Racks (R2 000/60 months)	R33	Monthly
Computers (R5 000/36 months)	R 139	Monthly
Salary - administrator	R6 000	Monthly
Maintenance - van	R 400	Monthly
Insurance - van	R 250	Monthly
Total	**R18 772**	**Monthly**

We now have a better sense of what it costs to run our business: just under R19 000 a month. Some of these costs are estimates. We do not know, for instance, if the maintenance of the van will be R400 every month. Neither do we know if the computers will indeed last us for three years without problems. That is yet another risk we are faced with in business and will need to manage; there might be a month when the costs will shoot up suddenly if you incur a huge bill for the gearbox on the van.

Our next challenge is to derive a cost for the product (the ream of paper) that we sell. We cannot do this without knowing how many reams of paper we will sell. In a way our transport (fuel) costs will be based on how many reams we will be collecting, hence how many trips we will take. But we can collect more than we sell, so we have to make an estimation of our sales. We have been dealing with this indirectly chapter after chapter when we estimated the market and our share thereof. If those estimates were incorrect, we are in trouble, and you will soon see how. This is another risk for us to manage. Now let us assume that we will sell 5 000 reams of paper. The initial exercise is to work out how much it will cost us to buy 5 000 reams of paper from the supplier. Let us say he charges us R10 a ream; therefore, the reams cost us R50 000 a month. Our costs then become R18 772 + R50 000 = R68 772.

Cost allocation to product

Now that we know that it will cost us under R70 000 a month to run the business, we need to translate this cost to the cost of the product. For this we need to be mindful of the two types of costs:

- the *direct costs*, those that are directly attributable to the product, in this case the transport costs and the actual costs of the products; and
- the *indirect costs* that are associated with running the business but not directly with acquiring the products, like the salary of the administrator.

We do this so that we can come up with the cost of the product from which we will make a mark-up and contribute that mark-up to the running of the business to earn a profit. It may not make sense at this stage since we have only one product, the reams of paper, to sell, but notice the significance of this later when we are selling more than one product.

Now let us revisit our cost structure and allocate costs to the reams.

ITEM	COST	NATURE	COST PER REAM (5 000 REAMS)
Reams of paper	R50 000	Direct	R10.00
Transport – fuel (to collect stock)	R3 000	Direct	R0.60
Rent for the office and warehouse	R7 500	Indirect	
Water and lights	R 800	Indirect	
Consumables	R 150	Indirect	
Vehicles (R30 000/60 months)	R 500	Indirect	
Racks (R2 000/60 months)	R33	Indirect	
Computers (R5 000/36 months)	R 139	Indirect	
Salary - administrator	R6 000	Indirect	
Maintenance - van	R 400	Indirect	
Insurance - van	R 250	Indirect	
Total	**R68 772**		

Each ream of paper actually costs us R10.60 to bring to the point of sale. Arguably, some costs, such as the maintenance of the van, are directly associated with bringing the reams to the point of sale. We need to realise, however, that the van does not only transport the reams. It is also used for other purposes such as, for example, going to the bank, visiting clients and visiting potential suppliers to do comparative pricing. This cost is therefore not directly attributable to the reams.

Setting a price for your product

Now that we know that it costs R10.60 per ream to bring 5 000 reams to the point of sale, and that it costs us R68 772 to run the operation, we need to set prices that will enable us to recover these costs and make a profit. If we did not buy or sell any reams in a given month, we would still spend money on some costs like insurance for the van, the administrator's salary and rent. These are *fixed costs* (cost that will be incurred regardless of business activity). In this example, the fixed costs are all costs except for the reams and transport. They amount to R15 772.

If we sell 5 000 reams and incur R15 772 of the fixed costs, we need to recover R15 772/R5 000 = R3.15 from the price of the reams. Therefore at R13.75 per ream (R3.15 + R10.60), we are making neither a profit nor a loss if we sell 5 000 reams. This is called the *break-even price*. Below this price we will sell at a loss and above this price we will sell at a profit. If we sold each ream at R15.00, R13.75 and R11.00 respectively, our profit or loss structure would look like this:

ITEM	AT R15.00	AT R13.75	AT R11.00
Sales	R75 000	R68 772	R55 000
Less: Cost of sales (reams and transport)	R53 000	R53 000	R53 000
Gross Profit	**R22 000**	**R15 772**	**R2 000**
Less : Operating expenses			
Rent for the offices and warehouse	R7 500	R7 500	R7 500
Water and lights	R 800	R 800	R 800
Consumables	R 150	R 150	R 150
Vehicles (R30 000/60 months)	R 500	R 500	R 500
Racks (R2 000/60 months)	R33	R33	R33
Computers (R5 000/36 months)	R 139	R 139	R 139
Salary - administrator	R6 000	R6 000	R6 000
Maintenance - van	R 400	R 400	R 400
Insurance - van	R 250	R 250	R 250
Net Profit	**R6 228**	**R0**	**(R13 772)**

As you can see from the table above, at R13.75 the business breaks even. Any price above that will offer us a contribution to the fixed costs that will land us in a net profit situation. We have two options for making a profit:

1. *To increase our prices.* As you can see, increasing the price will immediately drop a number to the bottom-line net profit. Increasing from R13.75 to R15.00 in this case has given us R6 228 in profits. This must be done sensitively, as the market will obviously react to price increases. If the price starts getting ridiculously high, the market will not budge and we will not make the money we intended to make.
2. *To increase volumes.* We have made our assessments on a volume of 5 000 reams. If we leave the price at R13.75 and fight hard to increase our volumes from 5 000 to, say, 7 500, our gross profit goes up to (R13.75 – R10.60) x 7 500 = R23 658, giving us a net profit of R10 886. This, as you can see, is a very viable option for us.

Price and competition

We must never lose sight of the fact that the pricing strategy has to take into account the market and the competition and how they are pricing similar products. We have spoken at length about competition and the need to be cognisant of the prices out there. If the competition's prices are very steep, it gives us an advantage to play with our prices and be able to cover costs and generate nice profits. If, however, our competitors manage to contain their prices, we are in trouble. It means that our strategy has to focus on containing costs, e.g.:

1. Where can we source a cheaper supplier for the reams of paper?
2. How can we negotiate with the existing supplier for discounts?
3. How can we reduce our fixed overheads and lower the cost of running the business?

Anything else, and we will be out of business in no time.

Pricing for two or more products

The principle that applies to pricing for one product is really the same as if we were selling two, three or a hundred products. Remember that the fixed overheads or indirect costs come below the product price calculation. You have to isolate the costs that are unique to each product. A large portion of those costs will be the cost price of the product itself. Then you will have other costs associated with bringing the product to a point of sale, typically the transportation costs. You will find that most of these costs are shared among products. For instance, if you sell more than one product, you do not go to the supplier for the sole purpose of collecting reams of paper. You generally will go there to pick up paper, files, pens and other stationery items that you want to stock and sell.

When you have calculated the cost of the units sold and worked out a competitive price, you will derive an amount that each product line contributes to your overheads. Remember that those overheads must not be catered for by only one product line, otherwise it will become expensive and price itself out of the market. All product lines must contribute to the overheads of the operation.

Each price must be determined based on how many units of that product you are reasonably planning to sell, the margin of profit that you intend making in each product line, and the competitor prices. Getting this balance right will make the products fly in the market.

Let us assume we are no longer selling only the reams, we are also selling staplers and files. The planned units of sales per month and the costs from the supplier are as follows:

ITEM	UNITS PER MONTH	COST PER UNIT
Reams of paper	5 000	R10
Staplers	400	R16
Files	1 500	R5.50

We know that our van is big enough to carry this load in a month at no extra cost and we will not need another van or additional trips, therefore the cost of R3 000 will remain. The question is how we apportion this cost of R3 000 to each of these product lines.

A simple way is to allocate it according to the costs of the products as follows:

ITEM	UNITS PER MONTH	COST PER UNIT	TOTAL COST	% SHARE	TRANS-PORT COST
Reams of paper	5 000	R10	R50 000	77.34%	R2 320.20
Staplers	400	R16	R6 400	9.90%	R 297.00
Files	1 500	R5.50	R8 250	12.76%	R 382.80
			R64 650	100.00%	R3 000.00

What we have done above is a simple exercise to answer a question: "How much are we paying a month to transport each of these product lines if we are paying R3 000 in total?" The only easy way is to base this calculation on the cost of each product line as a percentage of the total cost and multiply it by the cost of fuel. For instance, the reams cost R50 000 while all the products cost R64 650, therefore the reams contribute 77.34% to the total product costs. Thus the reams contribute the same percentage to the transport costs, hence the R2 320.20 of transport we have allocated to the ream. There are many bases that we can use, like the floor space and allocating costs on percentages occupied by reams, staplers and files on the floor of the van, but I reckon we will really be complicating this unnecessarily. The same basis can be applied to the overheads. The principle here will be to allocate the overheads of R15 772 to the products on the same percentages.

From here we know the cost per unit including the cost of running the business, i.e. the overheads, to be as follows:

	REAMS OF PAPER	STAPLERS	FILES	TOTAL
Product cost	R50 000.00	R6 400.00	R8 250.00	R64 650.00
Transport	R2 320.20	R297.00	R 382.80	R3 000.00
Cost of Sales	**R52 320.00**	**R6 679.00**	**R8 632.00**	**R67 650.00**
Overheads	R12 198.00	R1 561.43	R2 012.51	R15 772.00
Total Costs	**R64 518.00**	**R8 240.00**	**R10 644.51**	**R83 422.00**
Number of items	5 000	400	1 500	
Cost per Unit	**R12.90**	**R20.60**	**R7.10**	

The table above informs us of what each of these units costs. You will notice that just by introducing new product lines into our business, we have dropped the cost of a ream of paper from R13.75 to R12.90. This is because this product line now shares the costs with other product lines, namely the staplers and files. The more lines we introduce into our business, the more effort it will take to sell them, obviously, but the cheaper each line will cost through the sharing of costs.

Now that we know how much each product costs, we can develop a pricing structure for each of them. As we did previously, we need to look at what the market sells the competitor products for and our expected margins from the products, and price them accordingly. What is wonderful now that we have diversified our product portfolio is that we can make up potential losses of one product from the others. In essence, we have more room to play with.

Let us see what the introduction of these lines will do to the overall business profitability. If we assume that we keep the price of the reams at R15 and we sell staplers and files at R22 and R10 respectively, our income statement will look as depicted below:

	REAMS OF PAPER	STAPLERS	FILES	TOTAL
Sales	R75 000.00	R8 800.00	R15 000.00	R98 800.00
Cost of sales	R52 320.00	R6 679.00	R8 632.00	R67 650.00
Gross Profit	**R22 680.00**	**R2 121.00**	**R6 368.00**	**R31 150.00**
Overheads				R15 772.00
Net Profit				**R15 378.00**

It is not a foregone conclusion that the more products you offer, the more you will make. Certainly every product that you introduce must make sense to the market and must complement the other product offerings for you to realise savings through diversity and volumes. You will recognise from the above example that the introduction of two extra lines (staplers and files) has almost doubled the profitability of this business.

Manufacturing businesses

What we have been dealing with so far is costing products in a retail environment, which is where your business buys to sell. It is certainly less complex than if you are manufacturing your products to sell. The principles are somewhat similar but the application is far more involved. If you imagine it for a moment, you still have the costs of running the business, namely your fixed overheads, telephone, rent, vehicle costs, administration, salaries, and so on. These costs would not change. What does change is that you now have manufacturing costs which you will need to accumulate into the cost of sales of your products.

Let us picture the example of a company that is involved in the manufacturing of tables. It will typically incur the following costs:

1. cost of acquiring and transporting wood;
2. cost of preparation of that wood, whatever that might mean to carpenters, such as smoothing it out and getting it ready for manufacture;

3. cost of assembly material, such as the screws, glue, etc.;
4. cost of finishing material, the gloss and matt finishes, etc.; and
5. cost of labour, the manpower that will be engaged to do all of the above.

We can classify these costs into the following categories:

1. raw materials;
2. labour; and
3. factory overheads.

Dealing with this in an in-depth fashion is probably a book in itself. For now, you need to be mindful that all of these costs must be accumulated into the product cost and the rest will follow as if you have purchased the product from a supplier. With overheads, a distinction is made between the normal costs of running the business and the costs of production. Costs of production, electricity in the factory, rent of the factory plant, etc. are part of the costs of the product, whereas other costs are dealt with as normal fixed costs which still must be recovered in the price of the final product.

Service businesses

There are businesses such as attorneys, accountants, architects and many others that render services for a fee. Here again the service must be costed appropriately to ensure that it remains profitable when quoted and sold. The primary cost here is time. Most, if not all, services require resources to spend a certain amount of time working for or rendering that service to the client. Other costs will include:

1. travelling and accommodation;
2. telephone and other forms of communication;
3. printing material; and
4. other disbursements associated with rendering that service.

Again these costs must be accumulated and apportioned to the service to determine service costs. For instance, your accountants in the office are working on many jobs at the same time. What you will need to ascertain is the complexity of each job and therefore the amount that will be spent on it, and assign the cost of the accountant (salary) to that job to determine how much it will cost to perform and deliver on it.

Problems with costing

My experience in dealing with many small to medium-sized businesses is that they actually do not accumulate costs, at least not systematically. Prices of the products or services are determined arbitrarily without consideration of the costs. A profit is almost anticipated but never known. Most believe that costing exercises are cumbersome and that one needs accountants to do it.

Prices are pitched against the market and not after consideration of costs. They have realised that the market, particularly government, will buy from the cheapest bidder and they want to bid as low as possible. You have seen from the examples above that certain costs are fixed; very little can be done around them except to recover them through pricing or to diversify product ranges and push volumes. When this does not happen, you will find jobs left unfinished and very unhappy clients. This dents the image of your company considerably.

Make sure that when you cost your products you do it right, particularly when asked to do a quotation for a potential client. Clients want to work with the known. As soon as you come back and say you wish to increase costs because you were not aware of one, two and three, you lose credibility and fall out of favour with the client.

CHAPTER 11

Marketing your business

> - How do I bring my business and products to my customers?
> - What do customers really want?
> - How do I make it easy for my customers to reach my business?
> - How do I market my business and products?

The risk for your business that we are trying to manage in this chapter is that of not attracting customers or losing customers because you are simply not responding to their desires. Remember, your success in business will be determined by how many customers you can attract. If you recall, in the second chapter we concluded that one of the key contributors to business failure is an inability to attract and retain customers. That is where the money comes from and that is where the biggest risk is.

In this chapter I want to focus on that individual who really makes your business stand out – your customer! We will discuss this in two parts:

1. How do you attract customers to your business?
2. How do you retain them and create loyalty to your business?

A myth that I want to debunk right up front is that we, as business people, can exist without customers, and that there are so many of them in any case. Even if one is unhappy, it is no big deal – there are millions of happy ones out there! We allow this attitude to stick in our veins to such an extent that we forget to count. Every time a client is unhappy, we claim that he or she is the only one. And another one, and another one . . .

In our discussion that follows, I would like to impress upon you the value of a customer or client. I hope that, at the end of this chapter, you will appreciate that your business needs to be doing one thing right, and that is attracting and retaining the customer base.

Moreover, you need to ensure that your positive attitude towards your customers permeates your business. Your staff must respect your clients as you do. Many customers are chased away not because *you* did something wrong, but because they did not get the treatment they thought they deserved from your staff.

Attracting customers

One of the hardest challenges that businesses face is to attract a stable and substantial customer base. The challenge is associated with the dynamism of customers and the fact that they have different and variable stimuli. The diagram below illustrates how varied customers are:

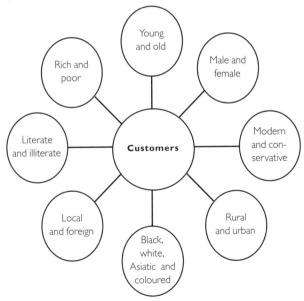

You will appreciate that the potential customer base is vast and diverse. In attracting customers you will have to take into consideration where they are to be found and what stimulates them. You have most likely identified your customer base in your business concept, so this should be relatively easy. For instance, young urban customers are found on the internet and in clubs. Old, rich men are found in the business newspapers. Urban, middle-class females will be found in magazines, soapies and malls. You need to know where your clientele is found.

The other challenge is to understand what stimulates your potential clientele, because that will determine the medium you will use to attract them. In other words, you need to understand the preferred medium of communication of your potential market. Rural people will be inclined to prefer audio means of communication. You can communicate your message to young professionals on the web while urban middle-class people can be reached through television. Other means of communication will include newspapers, billboards and flyers.

The third challenge is timing. The customers are not permanently in identified locations. They frequent their places of interest at specific times. Therefore you may not find them if your timing is inappropriate. For instance, television viewers will be available during the times that soapies are screened, mall visitors on Saturdays and on public holidays, internet visitors generally visit during working hours, and so on. You will need to know when your audience will be available. Sending your message at incorrect times will not catch their attention because they are simply not there.

If I speak for myself, for example, you will never find me watching television except in the morning when I try to catch up with the news on eTV or the SABC before going to work. Then you will find me on SAfm right through the day as I go to work and as I move between clients in the car. Any advertising that happens in those media at those times will certainly catch my attention. I suspect I represent a number of people like me!

The following are the various means and options of advertising:

Radio stations	Brochures and flyers	Billboards
Internet	Magazines	Malls and shopping centres
Newspapers	Exhibitions	Television

There are various other options for marketing and advertising your business and profile. You should do a careful cost-benefit analysis when you decide how you should approach your market. Advertising space can be very costly and you should really look at whether your business can afford it and the benefits you anticipate to derive from it.

Initially you will find that the best form of advertising you can do is self-advertising. Be active, see the clients, make presentations, ensure that your business is registered in the databases of the clients you intend approaching. Print those flyers and distribute them to as many people as possible. Make sure that you and your staff have something to carry that talks about your business, and make it available in the market. As you grow and generate revenue, you can consider spending serious amounts of money on marketing and advertising your venture.

Consult advertising companies for more creative advertising and marketing ideas. They know the game much better than I do and can advise on trends and the best approaches to the market. Make sure that whatever option you go with is in line with the taste and direction of your business. For instance, I would not go for cartoon-type adverts in my professional accounting practice. I do not believe this would be in line with the image I want to project out there!

Retaining your customer base

Customers typically look for three basic things they expect from a service or product provider:

- cost;
- product quality; and
- service excellence.

Cost

We are living in very challenging times, where money is scarce. At present, people have insufficient funds to take care of their basic needs. As a result, customers are getting more and more cost conscious. They do comparisons of costs among the competition and will be inclined to choose a supplier that they believe is "cheap".

You want to be that supplier! You need to make sure that your products are reasonably priced in the market. The only way you can do that is to find out what the market prices are. What is the competition pricing the products at? Walk through their doors and do the comparisons; do this because your potential customers will be doing it.

The other "tip" is to try by all means to drive your costs down. That will give you the latitude to manipulate the prices. Negotiate with your suppliers; do not incur unnecessary overheads; hire the bare minimum of people that you need to drive your business forward, and do not take from your business more than you need. Make sure that the costs of running your operation are as minimal as you possibly can get them to be.

Remember, what will drive your business will be volume. The more you can sell, the more profitable you will be, provided your prices are in excess of costs. (Otherwise you are making a loss for every product you sell.) Consider the following illustration:

If I sell 200 bananas at a price of R1 a banana, I make R200. If I drop my price to 90 cents and sell 250 bananas I make R225, which is R25 more. I will have customers that believe I am very reasonable in my pricing and they will want to come to my shop.

Offer discounts to your customers. Have loyalty programmes and give out benefits to those who frequent your business. Give volume discounts to those who buy in bulk. Cost your products to the customer, ensuring that your pricing recognises the support you are getting from the customer.

Remember that businesses develop a reputation of being cheaper than their competition. This becomes an attractive selling point to such an extent that customers believe that they will not find the commodities at a cheaper price and will automatically buy. You want to build that reputation because it will allow you space to dominate the market.

I go to Makro with blinkers on, as I just believe they are the most reasonably priced outlet in the country. I never even pause to think that I might be wrong. They have built that reputation in my mind over time, and it is almost impossible to shake it off!

Product quality

Although we have said that people are price conscious, we cannot ignore that they are almost equally quality conscious. They know the danger of buying inferior-quality products that might need to be replaced soon, which will cost them more in the long run. If you sell to corporate clients, you need to ensure even more that your quality is right. They really do not want to waste time and keep crossing the same bridge. They want it done right the first time.

Do not fool yourself and think that a cheap price will compensate for poor quality, because it will not. Quality will always beat pricing. Get your quality right and attract the next customer. Invest energy in improving the quality of your product.

A mistake many people make is to launch with poor quality, fool the customers and get them to buy. Trust me, you will fool the first set of customers, make a quick buck and get out of business. When they find out, which they will, they will spread so much negative publicity about your product that you will spend the rest of your life putting out fires and convincing every guy that walks through your door that the "rumours" are unfounded! You *really* do not want that for your business. The converse is also true. If you get the quality right, you have just done free marketing for your business. Everyone will be talking about you. People will come storming through your door wanting that product or service.

My painter was a referral from a friend. I did not find him by looking through the Yellow Pages. He painted my friend's house and did such an excellent job that my friend referred him to me. I have referred him to at least five other people and his painting-service business is just increasing every day. Not because he is lucky, but because his quality is good. His work is visibly classy. I hope you get my point!

Service excellence

When it comes to client retention, service excellence is crucial and probably as important as quality. Clients develop a relationship with service providers or owners of shops. That relationship is generally based on the quality of the service that they are getting. They want to be acknowledged and treated with care and attention. They will buy because of that relationship. Clients will not want to disappoint you if you do not disappoint them. They will even feel guilty if they buy from someone else, because they know the service they receive from you.

A critical thing is always to be there for your clients or customers. If they are looking for a product, it must be available in your shop. If they require a service, ensure that they get it. If you are always there for them, they will always be there for you.

Be efficient in delivering the service. I once made use of the services of an electrician to sort out my wiring at home. He was certainly trained and highly experienced, and his CV spoke volumes about his capabilities. I found him reasonably priced as well. However, he never kept his promises. He was always going to come over the next day, then the next day. When the job was finally done, I was happy, but it had caused me so much inconvenience because I had to make sure that someone was available to give him access to the property, and then he would fail to arrive. The result – I will never use him again. He was unreliable and did not keep his promises. You do not want this to happen to you. Keep your promises, be reliable and be efficient.

Life will not always go according to plan. Your car will break down. Your daughter might get sick or there might be a critical issue in your personal space. You will be surprised to what extent your clients recognise and respect that. Make sure that you communicate with them. Keep them posted, as they say! Clients do not appreciate a service provider who just disappears without a word. They want to know what is happening, when you will resume the services you provide to them. Apologise to them. The truth is, you have caused them inconvenience. Put your pride aside and tender an apology. If possible and depending on the magnitude of the inconvenience, make special offers, reduce the rate, or extend the service for free. Make them realise that you respect them and that you recognise that you have inconvenienced them.

Lastly, develop a personal relationship with your clients. Do not ever be bigger than them! They always want to feel special, because they are. If your business starts to increase in size and you are no longer personally involved in the operations, find someone competent to introduce to your clients and ensure that he or she maintains that personal touch between your company and the clients it serves. Thank them for the business they give to you. Remember, they chose you!

Marketing

What is marketing? Many people have their own definitions of what marketing is, others say marketing is the same as sales, while some feel that marketing is just placing a print advert in a magazine. In the true sense of the word, marketing is a combination of most of the things mentioned above. It is all the efforts or activities that you put together to make sure that the targeted consumer/customer knows about your product or service. Your offering (product/service) needs to be available at the right price at the right place (distribution) where your target market will access it, and at the right time. Confusing? Let's look at an example:

If you are in the business of making and selling learner support material, you need to make sure that the material is available in your distribution centres (shops) in time before the school term starts, to allow everybody to buy the products in good time. It is also critical to have the right mix of stationery products, such plain brown paper book covers, novelty book covers, pre-cut covers, etc. to cater for the different stationery needs. Once you have the right mix of products, they need to be priced correctly at each point of distribution, taking into account what your pricing strategy is in relation to your competition.

Most books on marketing summarise marketing in terms of the "six Ps" that form the basis for a marketing plan. They are positioned as pointed out in the diagram below:

THE "SIX PS" OF MARKETING					
Proposition	Product	Promotion	Pricing	Packaging	Place

These are the key areas that you need to consider when building your marketing plan. They are closely interrelated and have to work in harmony like instruments in a band. The success of your product will be as strong as the weakest "P". For instance, a beautiful product that is priced correctly but packaged in an unappealing manner will not be successful. Similarly, not engaging in a strategy to promote a product that is well packaged, well priced and offering a brilliant proposition to the consumer will cause the product to fail, for they will not even know that it exists. I can go on and on, but the point is that these "Ps" must be in seamless balance to create success.

Let's briefly describe each one below so that you get an overview of what I am referring to.

Proposition

Proposition is what the brand promises to offer the consumer. Generally this is viewed in terms of the product performance and whether the brand delivers on its promise. For example, people who purchase diesel engine cars primarily buy them for fuel consumption efficiency, and they know how much mileage they will get from one tank of diesel. If the car does not deliver on its promise and does less mileage than expected on one tank of diesel, the drivers will feel misled and robbed of their investment. This will have serious consequences: it will damage the equity of the brand of car and even threaten potential future sales. Similarly, when people buy toothpaste, they focus on a brand that promises white, strong teeth. Bio-Oil consumers are promised a smooth, healthy skin with all marks removed. It is imperative that your company or brand delivers on its promise, otherwise it will run the risk of destroying itself in the market.

Once you know what the proposition or promise of your brand is, make sure you that you publicise it. We will discuss this in the Promotion phase of the "six Ps".

Product/Service

Your product or service needs to address a specific need or gap in the market or provide convenience that is innovative and thus attractive to your market.

In the previous examples, we had a gap in the market where there was a genuine need: needs such as fuel economy, the removal of body scars, healthy teeth. As a result of these needs, people have come up with products: a diesel engine car, Bio-Oil, and wonderful toothpaste. Unless there is that product that solves the problem or finds space in the market, there is nothing to move forward on. It is therefore important to ensure that you locate or make that product to be successful.

I remember the days when accountants still wrote transactions in manual journals, when letters and documents were typed on typewriters. The world was cumbersome, documents untidy and errors unbelievable. You really had to be super-neat and concentrate to death to come up with a document that was not crossed for some mistake. There was a need in the market. He who identified it was bound to make money! The advent of Microsoft Word and Microsoft Excel as products was the beginning of these rands and cents flowing into someone's pocket. Need I say more?

Packaging

What are the various options of packaging your product or service that you are providing to your consumers/end users? Your can tailor-make your services to fit in with the needs of who the target market will be, and you can only do that when you have a clear understanding of who your key market segments are and what their key needs are.

The local telecommunications companies were very innovative in introducing a "pay as you go" package for people who do not qualify for cellphone contracts. SMSs and "call-backs" are quite popular in our local market and these were developed solely for the purposes of meeting the needs of those who have limited disposable income but want to stay connected. Another great example will be the spa treatment centres where you get various packages to suit your budget. It is vitally important to understand your target market so that your product or service is packaged in a way that will suit their needs. This could easily be done through market research. There are many ways of researching your target market even on a shoestring budget, for instance by observing the group of consumers and finding common needs, or surveying opinions through focus groups or structured questionnaires.

A friend of mine runs a highly successful funeral parlour. Part of his success is due to the fact that he has different packages from which clients can choose. For instance, he has what he calls a "one stop shop" package where you come in and, at a fee, have the funeral of your relative or friend arranged from beginning to end. You really do not have to do anything except show up like everyone else. Then he has other packages where, as the services are reduced, the price drops accordingly. The idea is that he has packaged his product to fulfil the varying needs of his customers. If he did not have a "one stop shop" package, he would lose some customers, as people are so busy nowadays that they hardly can find time to run around and prepare for funerals.

Packaging also means the appeal of the physical package in which the product is wrapped or presented. This takes into account the size and the nature of the packaging. Green packaging for foodstuffs, for instance, signifies nature and therefore health. A black packet would repel a yoghurt buyer! Ensure that the package in which your product is put is appropriate for your product and what it stands for. Would you buy fresh milk if it was in a black container?

Pricing

This is how much you want to charge for your product or your service. You have to take into account your margin aspirations per R1 that you invest in your business. That is, of every R1 you invest, how much will you get to invest back into your business to grow it further? Factors affecting your margins will include how you structure your pricing and the need to factor in the industry norm. Pricing relativities are also essential in your various packages. For instance, as a new entrant into the market you would want to drive awareness and trial, and get people to use your services or products. You would want to get as many people as possible to try out your product, therefore you would have special entry-level pricing which will potentially be at a discount to attract higher levels of sales than normal. A word of caution, though, would be not to compromise on the quality of your business offering; however, you will get less in terms of your bottom line.

In Chapter 10 we discussed product costing. You may want to interpret this discussion with the discussion on product costing, as the ultimate price for your product must ensure that you sell above the cost but in line with the competition. There is a point below which you will sustain losses, as was explained in Chapter 10. Similarly, there is a price above which you will lose sales to your competitors. You need to strike a balance.

I visited a shop that sells Bose Sound Systems, one of the best that I have ever seen. Unbelievably expensive! When I tried to negotiate, as I wanted a set, I used a technique that bounced back badly. I mentioned some brands that were much cheaper and said to the owner, "I might as well go to them and get this set at half the price!", to which he replied, "Go my friend, for half the price, you will get half the product and half the quality!" He was so sure of his product that he knew his pricing, although steep, was just right. His business is still operational!

Promotion

Promotion covers the various activities aimed at how best to communicate your product or services to your potential customers. We all know that marketing support spend is generally limited. It should therefore be channelled to areas of media where you as a business person expect to get the most returns out of your investment. A deeper understanding of the group of people you want to direct your marketing efforts to is key. For instance, what is the best advertising medium for these groups of people, and what is the key message that you would like them to take out of your marketing communication? When is the best time to talk to them? The last important question you have to tackle is: How do you want to talk to them? The "how" will be guided mostly by your marketing objectives coupled with the amount of investment you are prepared to put behind your activities. I have outlined some communication methods below for guidance.

COMMUNICATION MEDIA	EXAMPLES
Print	Magazines, daily and weekly newspapers
TV/Cinema	Targeting TV programmess of interest and movies
Outdoor	Posters in train stations, billboards on highways
Ambient media	TBC
Radio	
Public relations	Press releases, events, public appearances
In store	Promoters, posters, sampling, customer media

A product or service that is not promoted is not known. If people do not know about it, they will not buy it, however good it may be. Whatever you do, find some ways, and money, to promote your product. Many business people I have interacted with find this spend wasteful and unnecessary. I believe it is short-changing your beautiful product not to promote it and put it in the public eye.

Place

This relates to where your potential consumers expect to find your product or service. There are various distribution channels that you could consider. These may include direct selling (the internet, call centre or face to face), business-to-business marketing, retail chains, convenience shops at petrol stations, and so on. An essential component at your distribution point is branding, especially if you are a new entrant in the category of products and people do not know much about your offering. Yet another important element to consider at this point is, who is doing the purchase? Is it the end user, or is it a different person? Understanding these dynamics will help to guide you in what promotional methods you can use at the various distribution points to encourage people to try your offering. For example, the shoppers who buy disposable nappies are generally mothers. All your marketing efforts need to be directed to mothers with small babies and expectant mothers to drive awareness of your new range of disposable nappies and to persuade them to try your product.

To summarise: what we have looked at briefly above is known as the "six Ps" of marketing, which are basically the key areas that you need to cover when working on your marketing plan for your business.

Segmentation analysis

We all know that people in general are diverse and different, as discussed at the beginning of this chapter when we looked at the diversity of customers. In putting together your marketing strategy and ultimately your marketing plan you clearly need to understand exactly who your core target market it. As I have mentioned above, marketing budgets are limited. To focus your spend better, you have to be very sure of who you are targeting and what their needs and preferences are at that point in time. People's needs also change over time, and you as a business person need to be in touch with how the needs are evolving and to stay close to the latest local and international trends in your market. This will help you stay ahead of the opposition.

The exercise of clustering consumers into smaller defined groups or segments is known as segmentation analysis. Let's use an example to clarify this point. If you are marketing a brand of premium 4x4 motor vehicles, you will potentially have four different subgroups, which together form your entire market:

Segment 1: Young, ambitious, professional white men aged 25-35 who seek to drive a 4x4 car as a status symbol to reflect their career success to their childhood friends, colleagues and families. They read many magazines, including car magazines, and have access to the Internet, mostly at work. Keeping fit is an essential part of their lives, and they play a lot of sport and regularly watch sports programmes on TV. We can call this market segment *Ambitious Andys*.

Segment 2: Older African men aged 50-65 who are about to retire or have recently retired and who want the 4x4 as a reward to themselves for their life-long hard work. They read the daily newspapers and Sunday papers to catch up on some of the key highlights that they might have missed during the week. While they are highly progressive, educated individuals, they still listen to vernacular radio stations and watch TV programmes that cover current affairs and include national and international news. We will call them *Retiring Siphos*.

Segment 3: Married women aged 30-40 who are house executives and have young children, and are looking for big, safe vehicles for their travelling needs, which include moving around to run errands as well as transporting their children. Their interests include watching soapies, reading lifestyle magazines and going to the movies. We will refer to this segment as *Young Mothers*.

Segment 4: Single, ambitious, career-driven women aged 25-35 who hold high positions in male-dominated industries and are trying to fit into a "man's world". They mostly do not have children, and feel that they can make it on their own and do not need a man to succeed. This market segment can be called *Career Nozibeles*.

Unless you can find a common message across the segments that will appeal to all of them, you will have to decide which segment is most important to put your investment behind. That will help you deliver on your marketing objectives and give you a good return on the money spent in your marketing efforts.

You have four different segments. You will have to look at the size of the opportunity for each segment and also at your marketing objectives that you want to achieve on your brand. The biggest segment is not always the best one to go for. As a business person, you have to consider the vastness of the task of communicating your message to the potential customers and convincing them of the merits of your product/service. The more difficult and massive the task, the longer it will take your business to achieve your marketing objectives. It would generally also require a lot of marketing investment behind your brand.

Customer service

Customer service is another essential part of your business that you need to incorporate in your planning. This is basically a barometer or measure of how you are doing. To gather information on how your business is performing, you can choose one or more of the following tools:

- Set up a toll-free telephone line that consumers can call to enquire about your business/service.
- Have an email address for people to send emails with their queries.

- Prepare short questionnaires at your distribution centre with a few questions for people to rank your product/service. You can provide a feedback box in the stores or otherwise set up a free-postal reply service.
- You can build up a database of all people buying your products or people coming through your service centre and send out an email with a brief questionnaire.
- To have an effectively running customer service department, you need to ensure that your team working for you is:
    - knowledgeable and well trained in your business offering and what your business is all about;
    - trained in how to deal with angry and unhappy customers and solve their problems;
    - able to provide quick and direct responses to queries and complaints. Delays are a reflection of a lack of seriousness and lack of concern for the customer.

A poor response from your customer service team might have serious negative consequences for your business.

CHAPTER 12

Employing people

- How do I find the right people for my business?
- How do I enter into contracts with them?
- How do I formalise my relationship with my workers?
- What are the laws that I must comply with?
- What if I have the wrong person in my business?

In this chapter I hope to impress upon you that engaging people in your venture is much more serious than engaging assets like machines and vehicles. Being an employer comes with many demands that you should be aware of, and employing people cannot be taken lightly. You will need to ensure that your business complies with strenuous legislative requirements. Penalties are not only financial, but also social.

The basic premise when you employ people should be: *"Do unto others as you would have them do unto you!"* If we work from this premise, it makes a lot of things easy for us as business people. You will earnestly employ and lead people from your conscience, and the decisions you take about them will not conflict with your conscience and can be validated for fairness and consistency. Also take note that people can sometimes disappoint you tremendously. In such cases you need to take decisive action in the interest of your company and your other employees.

The diagram below depicts the employment cycle. In this chapter I will cover the elements of the employment cycle and give you some valuable tips on how you can best deal with each of them.

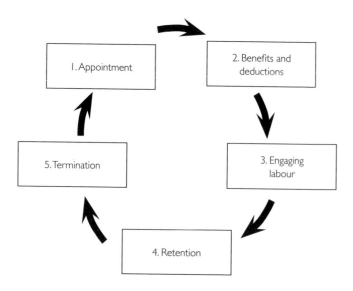

South African employment legislation

You need to be aware at the outset that the employment legislation in South Africa can be viewed by many as pro-labour. It is predicated on the fact that the workers are basically powerless (except if mobilised as a group) and can be abused by the capitalists for financial gain. The laws that exist seek to protect predominantly the rights of labour and to ensure that workers are not exploited in the workplace. There are a number of laws that govern the relationship between you as the employer and your employees. In this chapter I will focus mainly on one that I believe is absolutely critical for you as an employer to aware of: the Basic Conditions of Employment Act (BCEA).

Before I venture into it, I believe it is imperative that you have an overview of the Labour Relations Act (LRA), which governs the overall relationship between the employer and the employee. The LRA recognises that employees have the power to negotiate with employers only if they are organised into a bargaining unit, e.g. a trade union or a workplace forum. It therefore gives employees the right to organise themselves into such trade unions and gives employers an obligation to recognise them if certain criteria are met. This Act further gives employees the right to engage in lawful strikes (strikes that satisfy certain requirements) if they are distressed and employers are not conforming to their demands. The LRA also regulates the establishment of independent dispute resolution mechanisms including conciliation and arbitration as means to resolve conflicts in the workplace. As a final recourse, the Act regulates the establishment of a Labour Court and a Labour Appeal Court as superior courts to decide on matters pertaining to employer–employee relations.

Other pieces of legislation that are pertinent to the relationship that you will have with the employees include:

- the Employment Equity Act;
- the Occupational Health and Safety Act;
- the Unemployment Insurance Contributions Act;
- the Skills Development Act; and
- the Skills Development Levies Act.

The Department of Labour has published on its website all the various pieces of legislation that are pertinent to employment relationships. It is important that you, as an employer, constantly look at these pieces of legislation, as they may change from time to time.

Appointment

This is probably the most critical stage of the employment cycle. It is the start of a relationship. Once again, as with any partnership, remember that the employment relationship can be terminated but it comes with great emotional pain and financial implications. It is therefore important that you start the relationship on the right note. Engaging the wrong person is what you want to avoid by all means.

We often forget the "softer" issues when we engage people and focus only on the technical aspects, such as their ability to perform plumbing jobs, their experience as artisans, their typing skills, etc. We need to realise that our employees are often the face and the image of our business, the ones who are in touch with our clients in our absence. What they will present to the clients may determine what the clients will think and feel about your business. They can make or break your company. Personality therefore plays a critical role in employing people. Your employees' attitude, affability and compassion will motivate clients to do repeat business with you. These are some of the attributes you want to be on the lookout for when appointing people, not simply their ability to do the job.

You also need someone who can perform a number of tasks, especially at the inception of your venture, to save on costs of appointing more people. If you can find a plumber, carpenter or engineer with administration skills and a marketing flair, even better because you can ask that he supports your business in all these areas until it is sizeable enough to accommodate people who are dedicated to specific tasks.

It may seem very formal, but it is essential that you create a job description before you employ a person. A written job description has the following benefits:

1. It helps you to crystallise exactly what you need done, which assists in assessing what type of person you will need.
2. Together with the other job descriptions in your business, it helps you to establish whether there are any duplications, tasks that can be grouped together or tasks that are not really necessary. This streamlines your operation and gives effect to a very smooth organisational flow of operations.
3. It helps your employees to have direction and to know exactly what is required of them.

You need to make sure that you subject prospective employees to an interview process to assess whether they will fit into the job you want done. In this regard, it is imperative that you wear many hats when assessing an applicant: one, that of the clients who will be dealing with him/her; two, that of the fellow workers that he/she will be interacting with on a daily basis; and three, that of yourself and other supervisors that he/she will be taking instructions from. As mentioned earlier, you are not only concerned with technical skills here; everything about him/her is vital.

Do make use of references. Find out why the applicant left his/her previous employ and ask why he/she wants to join you. Their answers here will reveal a lot about their attitude and work ethic. Look out very closely for contradictions in their responses. Lies have a tendency of being inconsistent. Approach their previous employers, obviously with their permission, to establish how their behaviour was. There is a chance that some dirty linen might be revealed. Make them sign declarations that, if proven to be untrue, you may use to dismiss them. For instance, they must declare that they have not been convicted of serious crimes that may pose a threat to your business. Please note that I am certainly not discriminating against convicted fraudsters. Obviously they have paid for their crimes, but the fact that they have a record of this nature is something that you are most definitely entitled to know!

Benefits and deductions

The appointment will culminate in a formal letter that must be signed by the employee. Small Business still suffers from a sickness of not formalising appointments. This may have long-term repercussions for you and your business, particularly when disputes arise and the relationship goes sour. Make sure that every employee that you have engaged has a signed contract of appointment with the company. Such an agreement will spell out the following:

1. the position in which the person has been engaged;
2. the remuneration and allowances;
3. the benefits that they are entitled to;
4. the office to which they will report; and
5. other material terms of engagement.

Benefits

As an employer, you have an option to give benefits to your employees where such benefits are not prescribed by the Basic Conditions of Employment Act (BCEA). Those minimum benefits are obligatory in terms of the law but you are free to extend them beyond the required limits. The table below gives some guidance on the benefits that are prescribed by the Act. Make sure that you comply!

Employees are entitled to basic remuneration. They have worked for it and they deserve it. It is not a gift, as some employers sometimes imply when they drum it into the employees that they are accorded a favour by being employed. They have given you value and you would not be in business if it were not for them. If they have not given you value, you have avenues to explore to rectify the situation, but certainly they should not have to beg for their pay cheque at the end of the month. The fact that you have not been paid by your customers or that a machine broke down has very little to do with your employees. You decided to get into business, and you should absorb those risks. Obviously you want to have the kind of relationship with your employees where they can support you in difficult times like these, but that must be by mutual agreement, not because you are giving them ultimatums.

As indicated, other benefits that are stipulated in the BCEA include the following:

Meal intervals	• An employee must have a meal interval of 60 minutes after five hours' work. • A written agreement may — (a) reduce the meal interval to 30 minutes; (b) dispense with the meal interval for employees who work fewer than six hours on a day.
Annual leave	• Employees are entitled to 21 consecutive days' annual leave or by agreement, one day for every 17 days worked or one hour for every 17 hours worked. • Leave must be granted not later than six months after the end of the annual leave cycle. • An employer must not pay an employee instead of granting leave except on termination of employment.
Sick leave	• An employee is entitled to six weeks' paid sick leave in a period of 36 months. • During the first six months an employee is entitled to one day's paid sick leave for every 26 days worked.

	• An employer may require a medical certificate before paying an employee who is absent for more than two consecutive days or who is frequently absent.
Maternity leave	• A pregnant employee is entitled to four consecutive months' maternity leave. • A pregnant employee or an employee nursing her child is not allowed to perform work that is hazardous to her or her child.
Family responsibility leave	• Full-time employees are entitled to three days' paid family responsibility leave per year, on request, when the employee's child is born or is sick, or in the event of the death of the employee's spouse or life partner, or the employee's parent, adoptive parent, grandparent, child, adopted child, grandchild or sibling. • An employer may require reasonable proof.

Deductions

Like benefits, there are deductions that are stipulated by law that employers have to make from the salaries and wages of the employees. Any other deductions must be agreed upon between the parties before they can be effected. The BCEA is once again very clear in stipulating the circumstances under which employers can effect deductions from the pay of their employees:

Deductions and other acts concerning remuneration	• An employer may not deduct money from an employee's remuneration unless: (a) the employee agrees in writing to the deduction of a specific debt; and (b) the deduction is made in terms of a collective agreement, law, court order or arbitration award. • A deduction in respect of damage or loss caused by the employee may only be made with agreement and after the employer has followed a fair procedure. • Employers must pay deductions and employer contributions to benefit funds to the fund within seven days.

It goes without saying that you cannot just arbitrarily deduct money from Mandla's account because he broke a window of your car. You have to get his consent to make that deduction. Employers have a tendency to do this and, be warned, it is against the law. You need to have a policy in place for such circumstances and ensure that it is agreed upon between you and your employees. Follow that policy to the letter when effecting deductions. Also ensure that the employee concerned is forewarned and is expecting the deduction to be made from their salary.

Statutory deductions are, however, different in this regard and must be made even without the consent of the employee. Deduction of income tax, for instance, is one such deduction and must be made even without consent. (We will deal with this in the section on employees' tax in Chapter 15.) Other deductions are as per the requirements of the BCEA where, for instance, an order of court (e.g. garnishee order) compels you as an employer to deduct an amount from the employee's pay and pay it over to a nominated authority or beneficiary. Another case is where the employee belongs to a trade union and in terms of a collective agreement with the trade union, dues will be deducted from the employee's pay and paid over to the union.

Take note that employees need to be protected against the risk of unemployment in terms of the Unemployment Insurance Contributions Act. In this regard, an employer must deduct an amount equal to 1% of the employee's pay, match it rand for rand, and pay this amount over to the Unemployment Insurance Fund (UIF). This is intended to offer protection to employees in the event that they are retrenched and unemployed. Ensure that your employees are adequately registered and protected, because you do not know what the future holds for you, your business and, most importantly, them!

Engaging employees

Employees are not slaves and should not be treated as such. Remember the golden rule I referred to at the start of this chapter. "Do unto others as you would have them do unto you." Always keep in mind that they are a critical element of your business. As said before, they can make or break it. If they feel that you care about them, they will do anything to see you succeed. If they feel that you do not care, on the other hand, they lose interest in and compassion with you and your business. In the end – everybody loses!

The BCEA is prescriptive about how you have to engage your employees in your business. Remember, these are the *basic* conditions under which employees have to work. You are more than free to extend these and give them better conditions than the minimum required. In fact, it will do your business a world of good if you do so.

Ordinary hours of work	• No employer shall require or permit an employee to work more than (a) 45 hours in any week; (b) nine hours in any day if an employee works for five days or less in a week; or (c) eight hours in any day if an employee works on more than five days in a week. • This is applicable unless there is an agreement between the parties.
Overtime	• An employer may not require or permit an employee (a) to work overtime except by agreement; (b) to work more than ten hours' overtime a week. • An agreement may not require or permit an employee to work more than 12 hours on any day. • A collective agreement may increase overtime to 15 hours per week for up to two months in any period of 12 months. • Overtime must be paid at 1.5 times the employee's normal wage or an employee may agree to receive paid time off.
Daily and weekly rest period	• An employee must have a daily rest period of 12 consecutive hours and a weekly rest period of 36 consecutive hours, which, unless otherwise agreed, must include Sunday.

| Pay for work on Sundays | • An employee who occasionally works on a Sunday must receive double pay.
• An employee who ordinarily works on a Sunday must be paid at 1.5 times the normal wage.
• Paid time off in return for working on a Sunday may be agreed upon. |
|---|---|
| **Night work** | • Employees who work at night between 18:00 and 06:00 must be compensated by payment of an allowance or by a reduction of working hours, and transport must be available.
• Employees who work regularly after 23:00 and before 06:00 the next day must be informed of –
(a) any health and safety hazards; and
(b) the right to undergo a medical examination. |
| **Public holidays** | • Employees must be paid their ordinary pay for any public holiday that falls on a working day.
• Work on a public holiday is by agreement and paid at double the rate.
• A public holiday may be exchanged with another day by agreement. |

Retention

Diligent, knowledgeable and interested people are very hard to find. Businesses are battling with this issue every day. In South Africa we constantly hear about the shortage of skills and the lack of a dedicated workforce. Many people have developed a "rights culture", and a culture of entitlement has evolved in South Africa over time. Those who take responsibility and remain accountable are getting very scarce. The point is, if you are fortunate enough to come across one of these rare people, do whatever is in your power to retain them. Make sure that they are not lured away from you, which would place your venture in jeopardy.

The first tip is to realise that such people are not ordinary and should not be treated as if they were. Take cognizance of their special features and acknowledge them in your dealings with them. How you do this is entirely up to you. You may give a special thank you every now and then (which people always appreciate), recognise their value through pay, give them performance bonuses and promotions, or offer them a shareholding in your company so that they feel a sense of belonging.

For the rest of your employees and even prospective employees, create uniqueness around your business. The first place to start is to ensure that the conditions of employment are a bit better than average. You want them to see that the employment offering of your company is superior to that of the competitors, and make it difficult for them to leave because they will not enjoy the benefits they had in your company elsewhere.

Intensify training and up-skilling projects. Most people inherently want to improve. They want to learn new skills and, as such, will appreciate your company more if it offers them opportunities to learn and develop. Do make sure, though, that the programmes are beneficial to the company in the final analysis and related to the needs of your business. If you can afford it, offer bursaries and scholarships, take employees along to conferences and seminars, and invest in their intellectual growth.

Develop lines of communication with your employees. Let them express how they feel about your company. Let them teach you a thing or two about how best to improve certain processes and systems. It will help you improve your operation for a start, but will also make them feel valued in the company, and that alone will keep them closer to you and your operation.

Lastly, keep looking into yourself! Do not be above your employees. Do not isolate yourself from them. Remain close to your workforce and be part of them. You do have higher responsibilities and will be faced with situations where you have to prevail over them. Do that with empathy and ensure that although the stand you have taken may not be popular, it is one that they can understand and respect.

Termination

The painful reality about dealing with people is that even though you may treat them in the best possible way, there will be elements among them that will let you down. They will develop a culture of entitlement, abuse assets that you have invested in, steal from the company, be absent without your permission or be a general disruption to the vision of your company. Such employees need to be dealt with decisively and without delay, in the interest of many others that you have employed in the company and in the interest of the future of your venture.

Acting decisively and quickly does not mean acting recklessly or negligently. Remember that they also enjoy protection from abuse and discrimination, and they will play those cards when the going gets rough. You want to be sure that you have adequately protected your interests. Keep records of incidents, call the individuals to a meeting and have witnesses available when your reprimand them. Make them sign letters of warning that you issue against them and maintain those records meticulously. Most importantly, act consistently and within the framework of your developed set of policies.

The BCEA prescribes the circumstances and the manner in which we may dismiss employees from our operations. The following sections are particularly important in this regard:

Notice of termination of employment	• A contract of employment may be terminated on notice of not less than (a) one week, if the employee has been employed for six months or less; (b) two weeks, if the employee has been employed for more than six months but not more than one year; (c) four weeks, if the employee has been employed for one year or more, or if a farm worker or domestic worker has been employed for more than six months. • A collective agreement may shorten the four weeks' notice period to not less than two weeks. • Notice must be given in writing except when it is given by an illiterate employee. • The notice of termination of employment by an employer in terms of the Act does not prevent the employee from challenging the fairness or lawfulness of the dismissal in terms of the Labour Relations Act, 1995, or any other law.

Severance pay	• An employee dismissed because of operational requirements or whose contract of employment is terminated in terms of section 38 of the Insolvency Act, 1936, is entitled to one week's severance pay for every year of service.
Certificate of service	• On termination of employment an employee is entitled to a certificate of service.

Contract workers

Contract workers are an option that you have available to you, particularly at the inception of your business. You do not carry the risk of engaging them and do not have to pay the benefits as contemplated in the BCEA. Their engagement is regulated by a contract, signed between yourselves. They will perform functions as contemplated in the contract and any variation of their activities is a variation of the contract which effectively nullifies the existing contract and presupposes entering into a new one. These workers can be used in setting up your operation or in times when you need temporary labour because of unforeseen or temporary conditions in your operation.

Beware of falling into the trap of creating an expectation that a contract worker be deemed permanent by law, and thereby should enjoy all the benefits of your permanent labour. Contracts that are perpetually renewed can raise that expectation. Carefully assess the period for which you will be requiring the services of a contract worker, and engage them for that period.

CHAPTER 13

Financial administration

- What are transactions?
- How do I process the transactions into my books?
- What are accounting packages?
- How do I choose an accounting package?

What is financial administration?

Your business is a dynamic and moving entity. Unless you keep track of everything that is happening, you will not even know if you are making or losing money. Your employees are selling to customers and rendering services to them; suppliers are delivering goods; the landlord is requesting his rental; employees are looking to you for salaries, and the South African Revenue Service (SARS) is on your back! All of this is happening daily, hourly and even by the minute.

A businessman or -woman must keep an eye on the finances, but many never take the time to focus on this issue. Some do it only because it is that time of the year or month when SARS wants the numbers for tax assessments. Others will do it because the bank wants the numbers to give them a loan or overdraft, or a potential investor wants to perform a due diligence. These are not proper reasons for keeping books of account. They should be automatic when these parties require the business books, but they cannot be the reason for doing the books in the first place.

One extremely important consumer of the business books is you, the owner! You need to keep your finger on the pulse of the financial activity of your venture. This will enable you to take quick and accurate decisions before it is too late for your business, do informed analyses and have meaningful discussions with the suppliers and customers. Try to resist the temptation of focusing too much on production at the expense of administration. Right from the outset, I emphasised that business will consume a lot of your time and energy. Well, this is the area that you spend your nights on when everybody is asleep, the clients are not in your offices and production is on hold until the next day. You want to spend that quiet moment on your accounts and balancing the books. Depending on the size of your business and affordability, you will need somebody to focus on this for your business. Someone you can trust and who has the necessary skills. The point I wish to stress is: do not run your business blindly. You will wake up in the middle of a storm that you should have seen coming.

In this chapter I want to introduce the very basics of financial administration. If it were not a complex subject, there would not be chartered accountants who spend seven years trying to master it! It therefore cannot be condensed into one chapter by any stroke of the imagination. By the end of the chapter, though, you should be able to put together a very basic set of books, enough to keep control over your business's finances. It is advisable that you consult experts in the field when the dynamics of your business start getting complex.

Transactions

What your business is exposed to daily are transactions: dealings with parties outside your venture that have present and future financial implications. As explained above, these will include:

- buying stock on credit from suppliers;
- paying your wage bill;

- selling or rendering services to clients; and
- filling in your VAT return.

Remember that there is a separation of identity between the business and you. In other words, you qualify as an external party to your business. Money that you put in to revive your business is, therefore, a transaction that must be accounted for in the books of the business.

Transactions are classified into three primary categories, as depicted in the diagram below:

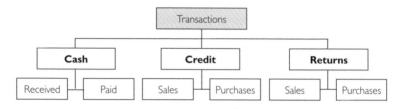

Typical transactions will be

- cash purchases or payments to suppliers, staff, and even yourself;
- cash received from customers as they pay for the services rendered or goods sold;
- credit sales, where customers promise to pay at a later date for goods or services sold;
- credit purchases, where your business purchases from suppliers with a promise to pay later; and
- return transactions that arise when goods purchased and sold on credit are returned and the debts owing reversed.

Flow of transactions through the accounting system

Transactions move systematically through the books, as illustrated in this diagram opposite:

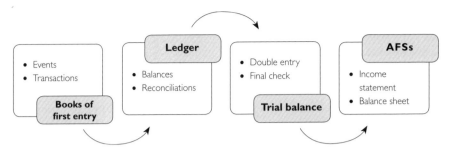

I will elaborate on this in the sections that follow, but, briefly, transactions are recorded in the dedicated books of first entry as they occur. They are then summarised into the ledger on a monthly basis. In the twelfth month, these are further summarised into the trial balance in preparation for the Annual Financial Statements (AFSs).

Books of first entry

When these transactions occur, they need to be recorded in the books of first entry. This means that your business must keep various journals to record the transactions daily as they occur. The following are typical journals that you should have:

Transaction	Journal
Cash Received	Cash Receipt Journal
Cash Paid	Cash Payments Journal
Credit Sales	Debtors' Journal
Credit Purchases	Creditors' Journal
Returns to Suppliers	Creditors' Allowances Journal
Returns by Debtors	Debtors' Journal

Types of accounts

Different accounts are created for different transactions, depending on the unique dynamics of your business. You need to analyse your business and determine the nature of the accounts that the transactions will be posted to. For instance, because you know that you will be withdrawing money from the bank to pay creditors and putting money into the bank as clients pay, you will need a Bank account to keep track of these transactions. Similarly, because you have leased the premises in which the business operates, you need a Rent Expense account to process all your rentals to. These are often called General Ledger accounts.

The ledger accounts are classified into the following five categories:

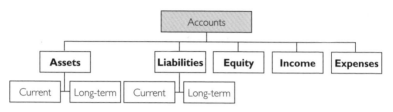

When transactions are processed, they need to be totalled to the accounts in the ledger on a monthly basis. This means that you should close the month for any transactions (which must be processed in the next month when they occur) and post the books of first entry to the ledger accounts. Let us briefly define these accounts:

- **Assets** are possessions of the business that have monetary value and are used to generate an income or to sustain the operations of the venture, e.g. vehicles, furniture, equipment, plant and machinery. They are classified into short-term assets, those that stay for a period of less than a year in their current value or nature (such as bank, debtors and stock), and long-term or fixed assets that last for a period in excess of a year, e.g. buildings.
- **Liabilities** relate to the financial obligations of the business, e.g. loans and creditors. Again, if an obligation is to be settled within twelve months, e.g. trade creditors and overdrafts, it is classified as current, while longer-term obligations are classified as such.
- **Equity** is the investment made by the owner into the business, including the profits made and invested into the venture, less any drawings by the equity participants or owners.
- **Income** and **expenses** are items of an operational nature that are generated and expended in the course of generating net profits.

Double-entry principle

Bookkeeping operates on a double-entry principle. In essence, this means that for every account that you debit there must be another one (or several) that you credit so that your books always balance. Different accounts will have different balances, which means that they increase on the debit or credit side. The simple questions you ask yourself are: "What have been the effects of the transaction(s) on the accounts involved?" and "On which side do the accounts increase?"

Going back to the types of accounts, the table below depicts where the accounts *increase*:

Asset	Debit side
Liability	Credit side
Equity	Credit side
Income	Credit side
Expense	Debit side

This table tells you that if, for instance, you pay rent for premises in cash, the two accounts involved are Rent and Cash. Rent is an expense and has increased by the amount you paid. Expenses increase on the debit side; therefore you will *debit* Rent expense. Conversely, cash, your asset, has been reduced by the payment. Assets increase on the debit side, but this one has decreased, therefore you will *credit* Cash. Your accounting will then "balance".

You will observe from the table below that certain accounts will always be involved for transactions processed in certain books of first entry. I have prepared this for you for ease of reference. Once you know which book to use to process which transactions, you will almost always know from this table which account to debit or credit. The corresponding account will depend on the transaction itself. Note that Dr stands for "debit" and Cr for "credit".

Transaction	Journal	Accounting Treatment
Cash Received	Cash Receipt Journal	Dr Bank
Cash Paid	Cash Payments Journal	Cr Bank
Credit Sales	Debtors' Journal	Dr Debtors
Credit Purchases	Creditors' Journal	Cr Creditors
Returns to Suppliers	Creditors' Allowances Journal	Dr Creditors
Returns by Debtors	Debtors' Journal	Cr Debtors

For instance, if I received cash from sales, the transaction I will process is in the Cash Receipts Journal. I will debit Bank (asset), as it would have increased. My corresponding credit will be to sales. If the receipt was for interest, the credit will go to the Interest (Income) account. If I was receiving payment from a debtor, the credit goes to Debtors (asset) account. In all instances I will debit Bank because the transaction would have been processed in the Cash Receipt Journal.

Reconciliations

In many instances you will find that as you process transactions through your accounting system, someone else is processing inverse transactions in their accounting systems. They are identical transactions, but only looked at from different perspectives. For instance, as you buy on credit, your supplier is selling (to you) on credit. As you pay, they receive. It is the same with the debtors, bank or loans. As you sell to a debtor, she is buying. As you receive payment, she is making a payment. Same transactions, viewed from different angles!

It makes sense, then, that at the end of the month, when the creditor or bank or any other party sends you a statement summarising their perspective of the transactions as they unfolded through the month, you "reconcile" those transactions with your perspective. You might find errors that they made and notify them accordingly, or errors that you have made and effect the necessary corrections in your books.

The trial balance

As the name suggests, this is a statement that summarises all ledger accounts and produces the annual totals. It also confirms the correct application of the double-entry principle. The total debts must always equal the total credits for you to know that your processing during the year was in balance. The trial balance will not necessarily pick up the errors for you to correct; the reconciliations are better placed to perform that function. The trial balance will merely notify you of a violated double-entry principle for you to track and correct. A typical trial balance will look something like the one presented below:

Trial Balance of ALMA TRADERS

	Debit	Credit
Sales		200 000
Cost of Sales	120 000	
Interest Income		15 000
Telephone	5 000	
Electricity	10 000	
Rent Expense	40 000	
Salaries	90 000	
Debtors	30 000	
Bank and Cash	65 000	
Creditors		50 000
Capital		95 000
	360 000	360 000

The income statement

We have already dealt with the income statement adequately in Chapter 7. Remember what we were chasing when we got into business: we wanted profits. Now is the time to see whether we made the profit we anticipated or whether we sustained losses.

Income Statement of ALMA TRADERS

Sales	200 000
Less Cost of Sales	120 000
Gross Profit	**80 000**
Add Other Income	15 000
Gross Income	**95 000**
Less Expenses	145 000
Telephone	5 000
Electricity	10 000
Rent Expense	40 000
Salaries	90 000
Net Profit	**-50 000**

This was clearly not a good trading year for Alma Traders. You are probably wondering what funded a loss of R50 000. If you look back at the trial balance, you will observe that the owners injected R95 000 into the business. Well, R50 000 has gone! The pains of being in business! They probably could have done it with fewer people and reduced salaries. Maybe they were buying expensively, hence their cost of sales, or they could have operated in a cheaper warehouse and reduced their rent expense. All of these are hindsight analyses that we can do of their business.

Balance sheet

Again, as dealt with in Chapter 7, this is a statement that depicts the financial position of an entity at a given point, generally on the last day of the trading (financial) year. Let us look at the one for Alma Traders.

Balance Sheet of ALMA TRADERS

EQUITY AND LIABILITIES

Capital	95 000
Net Profit (Loss)	(50 000)
	45 000

ASSETS

NET WORKING CAPITAL

Current Assets		95 000
Bank and Cash	65 000	
Debtors	30 000	
Current Liabilities		
Creditors		50 000
		45 000

It is clear that the owners have lost a substantial amount from trading. Although they have cash of R65 000 to settle their current liabilities when these fall due shortly, they will rely significantly on their debtors to pay and give cash reserves for their operations. The business has been hurt badly during the year, but the contributions of the owners are still enough to keep it going. If the pattern for the current trading period persists into the future, however, there will not *be* a future for this business!

That was not really the point here. I was just demonstrating the value of good financial administration when it culminates in reports and statements that can be used by the owners and assessors of the business when they make economic decisions about the venture.

Accounting packages

What we have been discussing about the flow of transactions through the accounting channel can easily be achieved by an accounting software package. I deliberately wanted us to have some discussion first so that you can understand better what accounting packages do.

Remember, do not invest in an accounting package if your business does not need it. And also take into account the anticipated growth and complexity of your venture before you decide on an accounting system to use. I will provide some guidance on what could work for your business in the table below, but the decision on how you want the transactions to be processed will really be yours.

Volume/Complexity	Method	Example
Low volume, low complexity of transactions	Manual	Manual journals from e.g. Walton's
Medium volume, low complexity	Spreadsheet	Microsoft Excel
High volume, medium complexity	Bookkeeping packages	ACCPAC, PASTEL Accounting
High volume, high complexity	Enterprise resource planning systems	SAP, JD Edwards

CHAPTER 14

Managing suppliers

> - How do I know when and how much to buy?
> - How do I get into contracts that win for me?
> - How do I assess my suppliers?

Managing suppliers is an aspect of your business that you must take very seriously. It can very easily determine your success or failure. The risk that is involved here, and that must be managed, relates to the relationships that you get your business into. How do you structure these relationships so that you win in business?

In this chapter we will investigate various ways of doing this. The basic idea is that any relationship you enter into must:

1. be cost effective for your business;
2. be efficient; and
3. give you the quality that you and your customers require.

Whether you are a service, manufacturing or pure retail outlet, your suppliers must meet these criteria. It does not matter whether you are supplied with raw material for the production process or just stationery for administration, the same principles apply. Every cost and every element of your business deserves attention.

Assessing your suppliers

A question that has always puzzled me is why people take time to assess their employees before they engage them, yet do not do the same with their suppliers. Of course it is much easier to get rid of an unsatisfactory supplier than to get rid of a worker, but by the time that you realise the supplier is not up to scratch, it is often too late. The customer is already upset with you. As we said in the chapter on risk management, prevention is better than cure. Assess your suppliers before engaging them.

Most suppliers will want you to fill in a form so that they can verify your creditworthiness and who you have accounts with. You should do the same with them. You want to make sure that you are dealing with a reputable supplier. You might not be formal and actually ask them to fill in a form but you need to be aggressive in your assessments. Find out what the size of their business is and whether they can handle the volumes of orders you will be pushing through. Enquire about the quality of their products, the people they are supplying, their guarantees and warranties on their products, and so on. By the time you engage them, you must be reasonably happy that you are not dealing with a fly-by-night supplier. You are engaging someone who will meet your requirements.

Where possible, ask for samples of their products. Enquire about the accreditation and quality standards that the products conform to. Visit their site and verify their existence. A friend of mine lost substantial amounts of money to a "supplier" that wanted a deposit before they could deliver, and then dashed off with it! He had relied only on the letterhead, which looked very authentic, and on a set of business cards that proved to be useless when he discovered that the address did not even exist. He paid the price for not screening his suppliers.

Make sure that you assess more than one supplier for the same products that you might require. In business all things are possible, including the shut-down of your sole supplier. His business may go under for some or other reason, and you are left stranded without alternative suppliers. Create a database of all of these potential suppliers and do comparative analyses of their strengths and weaknesses. Focus on one, but keep the others available as options. You might also experience an emergency where your supplier is engaged, renovating his business or closed temporarily. Call on the alternatives and get supplies from other sources without exposing you business to the risk of running out of supplies.

Developing a comprehensive supply strategy

What we suffer from most is the habit of buying in bits and pieces. You realise you need material on day X and you place an order, drive to collect it and use the material. On day Y you get told by your staff that there is a shortage of some sort; off you go again to place an order, collect and use. This we do so often in our private lives that it has moved into our businesses like a disease. It costs us more money in transportation and time, but, most important, it does not allow us to negotiate with our suppliers.

Let me illustrate with a very simple example:

If you took a taxi that costs R16 for a return trip to buy a can of coke which costs R7, the effective price of the can is R16 + R7 = R23. There is no way that you can attract and retain customers by selling cans for more than R23 to make a profit. If you do the same to buy two cans, you will still do one trip, therefore the effective price of a can will be (R16 + R14) / 2 = R15. The price has dropped tremendously just by going for two cans at a time instead of one, but you will still battle to sell the can for more than R15 to make gains. Going for 20 cans at a time reduces the price per can to R7.80, which is much more bearable in the market. All that you have done was to dilute the effective cost of travel to the volumes in order to minimise the cost of the unit. By buying more per trip, you have spread the cost of the trip across the products. All other costs, especially the cost of time, will behave the same way. Spending them on volumes helps you reduce the cost per item, keeping you competitive and profitable.

There are several things that you will need to consider before you decide how much to buy in one go. While it would appear to make sense to buy in bulk, the answer is just not so simple. A number of other factors have to be explored – let us look at some of them now.

1. **Space**

It will not make sense to buy items in bulk if you do not have storage capacity to accommodate them. Remember, items lose value if they are badly stored; some break or get damaged.

2. **Security**

It is always best to keep your supplies with the suppliers so that the risk of theft is not in your hands. The minute you move these items to your premises and pay for them, that risk is transferred to you, and you have to ensure that you provide adequate security for your products. Buying in bulk exposes you to a greater risk of losses, because if you lose, you lose more.

3. **Cash flows**

Money invested in stock is dead money! You cannot use it for any other purposes until you have sold the stock. You need to be very insightful when you decide how much to spend on acquiring stock. The more you acquire, the greater the investment and the more tied-up your money becomes.

4. **Inventory turnover**

This is probably the most crucial consideration of all. You need to monitor the movement of your stock constantly as the customers purchase, in order to determine how much you should keep. If your stock moves fast, you need to keep more of those commodities. Conversely, it would not be wise to buy 20 items all at once when you only make one sale in a year. That is why you will hardly find 30 BMW 7 Series cars in the dealership showroom on one day.

5. **Nature of inventory**

How much stock you keep at any one point in time will also depend on what you are selling. Taking into account the rate at which your items move and their nature will help you to achieve an adequate balance in your stock holding. Perishable items, for instance, lose their value over time, and if not sold, will be lost investment in stock. You do not want to overstock on these items. Similarly, seasonal items should not be kept beyond the season, otherwise you will be forced to mark them down in order to cut your losses and make them move.

We need to develop very creative ways of resourcing our businesses with the necessary material to operate and function. A thorough analysis of the number of contracts you have running, and an estimate of future contracts and the rate at which the material and products move from the floor would be necessary in order to determine:

1. the minimum stock that you should always be keeping on the shelves or in the production plant, and
2. the quantities of stock that you should have on order.

Minimum stock levels will be very helpful in ensuring that you are able to service your customers while you wait for the shipment that is on order. Keeping these levels is based on the rate at which items move in a day and the number of days that it takes for the supplier to deliver the goods to your shop floor. For example, if it takes 5 days for a supplier to deliver the ordered quantities of a product and you sell on average 50 of that product a day, your minimum quantity at any one time should be 50 x 5 = 250 of that product. The minute you have fewer than 250 and you have not placed an order, know that your business is in trouble. On some of the days you will have disappointed customers who came to support you and did not find what they were looking for. Have you ever been in a restaurant and ordered Coke and the waitress told you politely, "No, Sir, we do not have Coke in stock today"? Then you courteously change your order and ask for tonic water. "Sorry, Sir, we do not have that either!" You probably resolve there and then not to visit that restaurant again. What is the point of purporting to be a restaurant, you contend, if they do not have what people are looking for in a restaurant?

Determining the quantities of stock you should order is another science. You have to strike a very fine balance between overstocking and taking advantage of the economies of scale. On the one hand, locking your money up in stock is not advisable. Stock is, for one, more vulnerable than cash. Imagine that you have hundreds of hi-fi sets in stock because you placed a huge bulk order as it made financial sense to do so at that time. Then there is a break-in, or your staff disappears with half your products! On the other hand, it is cheaper to buy in bulk. Suppliers offer bulk discounts to encourage bulk buying because they obviously want to see their items moving off the shelves quickly. You are also in a better bargaining position if you buy in volumes. You can negotiate a price and you can wangle an early delivery.

So you need to strike a balance between bulk buying and overstocking. The following factors would probably assist you in your decision making:

1. *The nature and type of products on order*. Perishables cannot be kept in bulk, because you will simply be throwing good money away.
2. *The seasonality of the product*. Again, fashion items cannot be kept in large quantities. If they do not sell in a given season, they may never sell at all.
3. *Pre-ordered items*. If you have customers that have placed and confirmed orders from a catalogue, then by all means order in bulk. Those items will move and turn into profits as soon as they arrive anyway.
4. *The size of your floor space and warehouse*. You do not want to place orders for items that you cannot display or keep in a secure environment.
5. *Rate of damage*. Be careful not to order large quantities of sensitive items that break and get damaged easily. Rather keep that risk with the supplier and customer, and hold those items for the shortest possible time. If they break on you, rands and cents are breaking!

Negotiating with the suppliers

Once you have assessed and selected suppliers of your choice, you need to get them to the negotiating table. Earlier I dealt with how to go about deciding on your suppliers. Now we need to start deciding on how we structure our arrangements with them.

Once again we need to realise that they are in business and are in the game to make money and to make it quickly. As they negotiate with you, they will be putting their interests first, and so should you. Make no mistake, good suppliers will have your interests at heart as they will want to grow with you and retain you as a valued customer, in order for them to remain in business. Unfortunately, we would be naïve to think that this applies to all suppliers. There are those that would want to make a "quick buck" and vanish, and will do their best to milk as much money out of you as they can. Be smart and know the difference! You might wake up when it is already to late. Remember, you are running an ethical business. You do not want to be responsible for the downfall of others. When you are at the negotiating table, be fair but be firm!

The big question is: what are you hoping to gain at the negotiating table? Let us unpack this in very simple language:

1. Pricing

This is arguably the issue that should be uppermost in your mind when you enter into negotiations. Your costs (inventory, plant, machinery, rentals and equipment) *must* be driven down in order to make gains. You must have your prices to your customers in mind, and also the margins that you intend making, as you negotiate. You basically need to have your projected income statement with you and keep referring to it as the prices are thrown on the table. You must have a starting point for your negotiations and you *must* have a point at which you know that you cannot strike a deal with a particular supplier because it does not make sense. Trust me, she would also have done her homework and she knows where to start the negotiations and where to end them. At some point you will meet each other, and that is where the contract will be concluded.

Negotiate in such a way that it is worth their while to reduce their prices for mutual benefit. Your starting point is that you are a willing buyer and you have brought business to them. In this day and age they should be appreciative of that – business is not easy to find. Your next point may be the quantity of business you are bringing in. You have greater negotiating power if you are trading in volumes, because although the price per item may reduce to your benefit, the total value of money and profits is increased by quantities, to their benefit. To top it up, you are finding access into the market for their product, which will attract more customers for their ultimate gain. That is why products are generally cheaper when they are launched than once they are established.

2. Terms of payment

Your next critical point to negotiate is the pattern according to which they will be paid for their supplies. Here you need to do a serious cash-flow exercise. Always remember that you have merely bought stock, which will turn into cash only when it is sold and the customers have paid. Depending on the terms of payment you have agreed on with your customers, and your customers' payment profile, you might not have the money to pay your creditors when they require it. You want to delay paying your creditors for as long as you reasonably can. It sounds strange and a bit selfish, but you really want both their stock and your money as you walk in there to negotiate. Try and get both!

Be upfront. You do not want to get involved in legal disputes because you have not honoured the payment terms. Let them decide at the outset if they want to enter into a transaction where you will pay them, say, when your customer pays, or you will pay them in six equal instalments. Let them accept that as the terms of the relationship they have with you rather than build a bad reputation for yourself.

Understand their business thoroughly. You might be able to strike trade-offs for your benefit between the price and the terms of payment. For instance, you might succeed in negotiating a cash deal where you give them cash up front and they drop their prices. From their perspective, they have closed that deal immediately, have solved their cash-flow situation, and are free of the risk of having to chase after you to get their money. For that, they may be prepared to pay the price.

3. Terms of delivery

Here you need to negotiate that the items be delivered as close as possible to the point at which they will be sold or used. I cannot emphasise this enough: the game you are playing here is a cash-flow management exercise. You want the items to move as they are delivered, if it were at all possible. The items are costing you money while they are on the floor or in the warehouse, and they are also exposed to all kinds of risk. You need to negotiate that they are delivered just in time for use or resale.

Items that are financed through the banks are even riskier. Imagine a scenario where you obtain finance for racking for your warehouse, and the racking is delivered and paid for by your financier two months before the warehouse is available. Immediately, you are attracting interest to your venture, exposing your expensive racking to theft and other logistical problems, and just holding an asset that is not generating any revenues. Recovering from that mistake could cause serious cash-flow problems for your company. Make your assessments thoroughly and know when you want delivery to happen.

You need to be a bit hard as you negotiate about the terms of delivery. Remember, non-availability of these items can severely dent and compromise the image of your company. It might cause you serious headaches to try and recover from that loss of reputation, let alone earnings. Think of a situation where people go to your grocery store in the morning to buy fresh bread for their children's lunch, and it is not there because your supplier has not delivered. They might not come by the next morning for fear of being delayed when they have to drive to an another store and be late for work. You might gain a reputation of being unreliable. The question is, should you not fight to make the supplier pay for that? Building in penalty clauses forces the suppliers to be on their toes.

CHAPTER 15

Managing taxes

- What is income tax?
- What is value-added tax?
- What is employees' tax?
- How do I minimise my tax obligations?

In previous chapters I have referred in passing to various taxes that you as a business owner and an employer would have to deal with. I am almost sure that you experience a mix of emotions when you think of having to manage this aspect of your business: fear, anger, anxiety and possibly curiosity. How on earth does this work? What am I supposed to be doing here to minimise my tax burden and, most importantly, to be on the right side of the South African Revenue Service (SARS)? Well, I intend to explore all of that in this chapter. We will deal with taxation on income as well as other forms of taxation, namely employees' tax and value-added tax.

Why taxation?

This discussion is very important, even before we can get into the technical detail of how the taxes are calculated. A country has to operate and create an environment for its citizens to live in. We, in South Africa, are no exception. A road network has to be built and maintained for us to be able to move around. Public hospitals for our sick, schools and universities for our children have to be set up, staffed and maintained. The elderly and the vulnerable have to be taken care of, and so the list goes on. If we did not do these things as a society, we would be failing to ensure that South Africa is indeed "alive with possibilities" and "for all who live in it".

These tasks are, however, the responsibility of government. Ours as citizens is to support government primarily with creating and making funds available to discharge these responsibilities. There therefore has to be a system by means of which our government can get our contributions into its funds to work on enabling its citizens to live a better life. That system must also be regulated sufficiently to ensure that we can all make a contribution, and that nobody gets lost from the contribution net and ends up not playing his or her role in sustaining our country and those who live in it. That is the South African tax system. Many dislike it, but without this system, there would be no South Africa.

The South African tax system

South Africa has many types of taxation and, as mentioned, they are designed to give the state funding to operate and to fulfil its objectives on behalf of the citizens. The table below describes some of the tax types that you may be aware of and to an extent exposed to in your daily life. In this book I will focus only on those that have implications for your business administration and that you need to declare to SARS. (SARS is also referred to as the Receiver of Revenue or simply the Receiver.)

Income tax	Taxation that is levied on the income generated by a business or private individual.
Employees' tax	Taxation that is paid by the business or employer on behalf of its employees. This is deducted from the employees' salaries and paid over to SARS.

Value-added tax	Taxation that is levied on goods and services bought and sold.
Secondary tax on companies	Taxation that is levied on dividends declared by companies.

Income tax

In a nutshell, as the name suggests, income tax is tax on income. The income tax system in South Africa is progressively structured so that if you earn more income, you pay more tax to SARS. The table below illustrates the prescribed tax rates for small business companies:

Taxable income	Tax payable
R0 – R54 200	0%
R54 201 – R300 000	10% of the amount above R54 200
R300 001 and above	R24 580 + 28% of the amount above R300 000

Let us look at some examples:

- If your company generates taxable income (we will define this concept later) of R250 000 in a tax year, SARS will claim taxation of 10% of (R250 000 – R 54 200) = R19 580.
- If your company generates taxable income of R400 000, the taxation charge will be:

R24 580 + 28% of R100 000 = R24 580 + R28 000 = R52 580.

The tax year is a period of 12 consecutive months as determined by your business. For natural persons and trusts, this period ends on the last day of February every year. This is the date on which the returns and declarations of income and expenditure should be made to allow SARS to work out the tax implications of the business's trading and apportion tax appropriately. The business is then required to make payments to or entitled to receive refunds from SARS depending on these calculations.

This is how the system works:

Tax calculation

I will discuss this shortly, but first it needs to be said that the tax calculation is not entirely based on income but on *taxable income*. This presupposes that not all income is subject to tax. Well, what is taxable income?

> Gross income
> Less: exempt income
> Less: deductions and allowances
> = taxable income (the income on which your tax obligations are based)

Gross income

The first exercise in the determination of tax due to SARS is the determination of gross income. This is the total value of receipts and accruals that have been earned in the tax year. In simple terms, this is how much money the business has generated and/or received during the tax year.

At this stage it does not matter where the money was received from and what it was meant to be for. Therefore gross income includes any of the following:

- sales of goods and services;
- sales of equipment and other assets of the business;
- donations made to the business; and
- interest earned in the bank account of the business.

Basically, if it was invoiced out to customers or received from other parties, it falls into the calculation of gross income.

The next step is to isolate and remove all receipts from sources outside the Republic of South Africa and capital receipts from your gross income calculation. This means that from the calculation of the elements above, you would then exclude:

- donations made to the business;
- sales of equipment and other assets of the business; and
- any money received from foreign nationals.

These are not receipts earned in the ordinary course of your business. Unless you trade in equipment, in which case such equipment is your trading stock and not assets, sale of equipment is not regarded as a sale in the ordinary course of business. These are therefore receipts of a capital nature.

Exempt income

There is some income that we have deliberated on and accumulated above that will be exempt from tax. This means that the business will not be charged tax on this income earned. There are serious and vast regulatory implications with respect to excluding income from tax which I will not articulate properly in this chapter as they would constitute a book in themselves. The SARS website and personnel would give proper guidance in this regard. Some of the income that would be exempt from tax in part or entirely includes the following:

- interest;
- dividends earned; and
- grants from government.

In essence, this means that if your company had shares in other companies, for instance, the dividend that it would earn from that investment would not attract taxation. Similarly, if for some reason government advances funds to the company by way of a grant, those funds would not attract taxation.

Deductions and allowances

At this stage, you will appreciate that we have accumulated an amount of income earned and accrued to the company (gross income) and have taken away all income that would ordinarily not be taxable (exempt income), and are now left effectively with the income that SARS would tax the company on.

Now we need to realise that it has, in fact, cost the company some money to generate this income. In other words, there are expenses that the company has incurred in the process of running the business and generating such income. Taxing the company on the income without recognising that the company is already out of pocket, expense-wise, would be jeopardising the entity twice. It is for this reason that SARS recognises some expenses in the calculation of taxable income and allows the company to deduct those expenses provided that they were incurred in the generation of income. Therefore, if you were selling calculators and sold R500 000's worth in the tax period, you would not be taxed on the full R500 000. SARS would allow you to deduct costs incurred by you to make the R500 000, such as the purchase costs for the calculators, transport costs, costs of labour and storage costs. As long as you can demonstrate that the costs were necessary to conduct your business, and can provide authentic supporting documents for such costs, SARS would allow you to deduct them.

There are vast and complex rules with respect to deductions and allowances which I will not cover in this book, except to say that illegal transactions, fines and penalties are not expenses that SARS would entertain and allow you to deduct from income. Therefore, if you were caught and given a speeding fine, you would not be allowed to deduct the fine from your income, even if you were rushing to deliver a tender before it closed.

Domestic expenditure also constitutes expenses that cannot be deducted from income. Personal and family groceries, electricity and the rental for your flat cannot be deducted. If, however, you conduct your business affairs from your home, you are allowed to deduct "domestic" expenses that relate to the business from the income of the business. Therefore, the rentals, electricity and other utilities can be deducted to the extent that they relate to the business.

An important tip on deductions

Interestingly, most business people establish their businesses and operate them at times from their pocket. It is easy to become caught in the circle of spending from your pocket and wanting to see financial reserves (i.e. money) accumulating in your business bank account.

From a financial management point of view, it is important for any business to streamline its financial exposure or activities to its budget (operate within the set budget framework).

When you think about it, at the commencement stage of the business an entrepreneur is naturally very hands-on when it comes to operational matters (payment of accounts and buying of necessities) of the business.

Example

Xolani is an entrepreneur and runs a marketing and advertising company. Whenever Xolani pays his accounts, both personal and business, he pays them from his personal account because "he is his business, after all". This simply means that his monthly drawings from the business will increase proportionally to accommodate the added responsibilities. Where Xolani would ordinarily be drawing R10 000 towards his salary, he finds himself drawing R18 000 to accommodate some of the business expenses. This will result in Xolani's taxable income potentially being R216 000 as opposed to R120 000. The possible implications are set out below. (The mentioned example may not be applicable to a sole trader and/or a partnership business as the owner or partners and the business are deemed to be one taxpayer.)

- *Personal tax* – SARS expects of any entrepreneur to complete a provisional tax form for assessment of taxes to be paid. The actions in the above example would attract unnecessary tax on the owner as he would have increased what SARS would deem as salary earned.
- *Business tax* – the business would not be presenting a true reflection of the company's expenses that would ordinarily assist in the reduction

of taxable income. Furthermore, the business would not be in a position to claim any VAT that the company would ordinarily be able to claim, as these expenses were not paid for by the business. (VAT will be explained shortly.)

With just a simple exercise of operating within your budget framework and a bit of discipline in doing so (ensuring that business payments and expenses are paid using the business account), you would be able to tell how your company is truly performing.

Value-added tax

Value-added tax (VAT) is another form of taxation, which is charged on goods and services traded in our economy. The VAT system is structured in such a way that the person that eventually bears the burden of taxation is the final consumer of the goods and services. If, for instance, you are purchasing goods and services to resell, you are not a final consumer in the system and therefore will not pay VAT. If you are in that category, i.e. not a final consumer of goods and services, you are registered in the system as a VAT vendor; in other words, you are, loosely put, an agent or vendor for SARS, to collect taxes on goods and services on their behalf. Whatever VAT you pay, you will claim back from SARS, and whatever VAT you charge on your products or services, you will pay over to SARS.

Who is a VAT vendor?

Not everyone who trades is automatically a VAT vendor. The system and rules from SARS require that you must be registered within their system to be a VAT vendor. Such registration results in a unique VAT number which you must display to those that you will charge VAT on goods and services you sell, otherwise they are not obliged to pay you VAT because it stands to reason that you are not going to pay that VAT over to SARS since you are not even in their system.

All businesses that will be making taxable supplies in excess of R1 million in a 12-month consecutive period are compelled to register for VAT. This means that if you know that over the next 12 months your business will make revenue in excess of R1 million from the sale of goods and services, you are by law required to register for VAT. The law allows for voluntary registration, however, if you have been making revenue of a minimum of R20 000 over the last 12-month period. Later we will look at why it would make sense to decide to volunteer and register as a VAT vendor. This will be easiest when we have a full understanding of how the system actually works.

What are the implications of being a VAT vendor?

The most important issue is that if you or your business is registered either compulsorily or voluntarily as a VAT vendor, you are charged with the responsibility to collect VAT for SARS. This means that you will be responsible for declaring to SARS how much trading you have generated (value of goods and services bought and sold) and will pay or be paid the VAT associated with those supplies, depending on whether you have bought more than you have sold.

It then immediately places another responsibility on you: to be systematic and diligent with your record-keeping and administration systems as you have to keep close tabs on your purchases and sales, because these have VAT built into them. All purchases from suppliers where VAT has been charged must be recorded and the VAT recorded separately, as this VAT must be paid back to you by SARS. Similarly, VAT must be added to all sales you make to customers, and this VAT must be paid over to SARS as you were charging it on their behalf.

The system operates in such a way that you have to make these declarations of trading once every two months, and the VAT associated with that trading must be paid over by the 25th of the following month. The implications are that every second month you need to fill in declaration forms to SARS and calculate the VAT implications of your trading for the past two months. If that trading has resulted in your having collected more VAT than you have paid out, a payment to SARS must be made by the 25th of the third month.

Let us play with two simple examples:

1. You are in the business of buying and selling IT equipment and are registered for VAT. You bought IT equipment to the value of R25 000 and were charged VAT of R3 500 (14% of R25 000), which means you were invoiced for R28 500 by the various suppliers. In the same period you sold this equipment for R32 000 and charged VAT of R4 480 to make your total invoicing R36 480

   The R3 500 VAT that you were charged is called input VAT and the R4 480 is termed output VAT. The VAT due or owing is therefore:

Output VAT	4 480
Less: input VAT	3 500
Difference	980

   This means that your business owes SARS R980. You have raised more VAT than you have been charged.

2. You are still in the business of buying and selling IT equipment and are registered for VAT. During this cycle you bought IT equipment to the value of R50 000 because you were positive about the prospects of your business and were charged VAT of R7 000 (14% of R50 000), which means you were invoiced for R57 000 by the various suppliers. Things did not go according to plan and in the same period you sold equipment for R20 000 and charged VAT of R2 800 to make your total invoicing R22 800.

   The R7 000 VAT that you were charged is called input VAT and the R2 800 is termed output VAT. The VAT due or owing is therefore:

Output VAT	2 800
Less: input VAT	7 000
Difference	4 200

   This means that your business will get a refund from SARS of R4 200. You have raised less VAT than you have been charged. Somewhere in the supply chain the suppliers that sold you the equipment will pay the VAT of R7 000 that you have deducted.

Something worth noting about the system

The VAT system operates on an accrual and not a cash basis. This means that you will charge VAT on invoices you raise to your customers and you will be charged VAT on invoices you receive from your customers. These are the invoices that will be in the declaration to SARS and these are the invoices on which VAT will be paid to you or by you to SARS. The system does not operate on a cash basis in that it does not recognise whether you have been paid or have paid these invoices. It is therefore critical to note that there may be instances, and in business most likely, where your customers have been invoiced but have not paid by the time this VAT is due to SARS. Such payment must nevertheless be made to SARS.

SARS is entitled to charge interest and penalties if there is money due and it is not paid over. Be careful not to fall into that trap. The penalties and interest can be very substantial and can have a negative impact on the profitability of your business. Furthermore, as with traffic fines, you cannot claim these costs as deductions for income tax purposes. You had control over them, at least according to SARS, and they were not a necessary ingredient of your business operations.

Think carefully about this. You sold a computer worth R10 000 and charged VAT of R1 400 (making it R11 400) to a customer who took his time to pay you. You had purchased the computer for R8 500 and were charged VAT of R1 190, making the total invoice R11 190. The difference of R1 400 − R1 190 = R210 was payable to SARS but you did not pay it, attracting interest and penalties. Your profit for this computer is therefore R10 000 − R8 500 = R1 500. Remember that this is exclusive of VAT since you were just an "agent" for VAT purposes. If this VAT is not paid because you are waiting for the customer to pay you the R11 400, SARS will charge you interest and penalties for late payment. Trust me, they can be exorbitant. If these are eventually R100, you will have eroded your profit of R1 500 to R1 400, something that is not desirable to your business. The numbers in this example are quite small but, as your business gains momentum, these amounts can dent your profits significantly. My advice is – pay your taxes on time! "After all, it is the right thing to do!"

Claiming VAT

Business people often have the tendency to put all purchases into the input tax calculation, obviously to inflate input tax in order to reduce the VAT that is payable, or even to get SARS to pay them some VAT back. Other than the fact that this exercise can land you in a serious fraud case, there are certain items for which you cannot claim VAT. I will not get into the detail of what these are; please consult the SARS offices for guidelines. Typical expenditure where people try to play these tricks include:

- Purchase of vehicles. A person buys a luxury sedan for R800 000, is charged R112 000 VAT by the supplier of the vehicle and puts this on the claim, hoping to get the VAT back. This can only done in the case of commercial vehicles!
- Domestic expenditure. A person buys groceries and gifts for his wife or girlfriend, obviously gets charged VAT and slips the receipts into the VAT file, hoping that these will be recognised as business entertainment expenses, thereby reducing his VAT liability.

Input VAT receipts

If you are a VAT vendor, you need to comply with specific requirements on how your invoices should be presented. Similarly, when you pay VAT on an invoice for purchases and are hoping to claim this back from SARS, be careful that the invoice on which you will be claiming complies with these requirement, otherwise you may not be allowed to claim it back from SARS. The following invoice is a guideline on these specific requirements.

Details of the company, like address, company name, registration and VAT no.

Must state "Tax Invoice"

Client's details including the VAT No.

Your VAT calculations should be clear

Turnover tax

You will agree that the taxes that we have just discussed are not very easy to understand, let alone administer. The requirements are very stringent and most owner-managed businesses just do not have the time to pay attention to all this detail. The good news is that SARS has realised this and has introduced a much more refined taxation system to replace all of these. The new taxation is called turnover tax.

Turnover tax is applicable to all businesses that make a turnover of up to R1 million per tax year that voluntarily elect to move across and avoid the burden of tax administration. Unfortunately, if the turnover of the business is in excess of this threshold, the status quo remains, at least for now. In the new system, the business is taxed once on its turnover by applying the table below. Remember, the turnover tax consolidates and replaces the taxes that otherwise would be levied on capital gains, VAT, secondary tax on companies and income tax. Some of these taxes I have deliberately not discussed in this book.

Taxable turnover (R)	Rate of tax (R)
0 – 100 000	0%
100 001 – 300 000	1% of the amount above 100 000
300 001 – 500 000	2 000 + 3% of the amount above 300 000
500 001 – 750 000	8 000 + 5% of the amount above 500 000
750 001 and above	20 500 + 7% of the amount above 750 000

Employees' tax

This form of taxation is applicable to employees of a company. Here I will discuss briefly how the tax system operates and focus on the responsibilities that employers have in the administration of this form of taxation. If you refer to Chapter 12, which dealt with employment, you will recognise who the employer is and be able to determine whether you or your company is, in fact, the employer as defined. Loosely put, if you have engaged people in employment and are remunerating them for their services to the company, you are an employer as defined and you need to comply with the requirements in terms of employees' tax.

How does the system work?

Employees' tax is in fact taxation on income earned by the employees of an entity. Like income tax, employees' tax is predicated on the fact that all citizens of this country that earn income must be subjected to taxation and contribute to the revenue coffers of our government. The distinction with this form of taxation is that it places an onus on employers to deduct tax from employees' salaries and pay it over to SARS. The law prescribes that this taxation must be calculated and deducted from the remuneration of employees and be paid to SARS by the seventh day of every month. As with all taxation, if this is not done, there are severe penalties levied by the office of the commissioner. As a matter of fact, it is a criminal offence not to deduct and pay over this tax.

This was, in fact, introduced to ease the tax-payment burden on the part of employees and to give cash flows to SARS. Imagine if you had to get your full gross pay every month and end up with a tax obligation of R120 000 at the end of the year. You would rather bite this in chunks of R10 000 every month. It is better for you and for SARS.

Elements of employees' tax

There are two elements to employees' tax: one is Standard Income Tax on Employees (SITE) and the other is Pay As You Earn (PAYE). SITE applies only to employees who earn less than R60 000 per annum, do not earn other income and do not earn a travelling allowance. Normally they would not even be required to submit a tax return every year. PAYE, on the other hand, is progressive taxation that is deducted based on an employee's remuneration. The more an employee earns, the higher the deduction for tax.

There are mechanisms for calculating the taxation that must be deducted from employees, which I do not intend to discuss in this book. It must be emphasised that such taxation does not belong to the employee or the employer, but is due to SARS every month that it is deducted from employees.

An employer is required to issue an IRP5 certificate to each of its employees annually. This certificate basically details the total remuneration that the employee received in the tax year, including allowances, and the amount of SITE and PAYE that was deducted and paid over during the same period. This is the certificate that employees must put into their income tax returns annually to enable SARS to calculate whether the tax that was deducted from the employee was more or less than what should have been deducted based on their remuneration. That relationship is, in essence, outside of employment as it is between the employee as a taxpayer and SARS.

Skills Development Levy

South Africa is a country that wants to focus on developing skills in the workplace. A new levy was therefore introduced to ensure that there are available funds for skills development. The Skills Development Levy (SDL) is charged at 1% of the "leviable" or payroll amount, which is calculated using the same figures used to calculate PAYE. This amount is calculated after taking into account:

1. medical aid contributions for employees over 65;
2. retirement annuity fund contributions; and
3. pension fund contributions.

The wonderful aspect of this levy is that companies can claim some money back provided that they can demonstrate that they have engaged in allowable initiatives for training and development of their employees, so the levy is not money lost by companies.

Businesses and employers that believe that the "leviable" amount in any given month will not exceed R250 000 are exempt and do not have to pay the levy. This does not imply that they do not have to register in terms of the Skills Development Act. It only absolves them from paying the levy.

Businesses that are not exempt from paying the levy must do so within seven days after the end of the month in which salaries were paid to employees. Any failure to do so will lead to penalties and interest, which eat into the profitability of the business.

A final word

Life is, in essence, what you want it to be. The road you take is the one that you choose. Circumstances, challenges and turbulence do not choose for you the path you should take. They act as assurers that you are, in fact, on the right path. They act as major trophies on your achievements. We value that for which we work hard. We gain more recognition if we survive the pain of our endeavours. Trust me, if it comes too easy, maybe it is not worth doing.

There are many easy roads to money. Most of them at best lead you to prison, and at worst kill your soul, your sense of achievement and your pride. A road to success is hard, long and full of doubt and despair. It is rocky and cumbersome. But it is the road to success! Tackle it wisely, persevere, and seek guidance. But do take it! Your success will not only be felt by yourself, but will filter through to society and to the next generations. You will not only create wealth, but will build a legacy for yourself.

I said right at the beginning of this book that the success or failure of your business will depend on you. How strong-willed are you? How purposeful are you? How resilient are you? How empathetic are you to the needs of others – your suppliers, business associates, customers, employees and the general society? You will set the tone. You will determine the pace. You will take your business to great heights.

Be bold, be honest, and work hard!

All the best.

Appendix: Repayment Calculator

REPAYMENT CALCULATOR: 1–20 MONTHS

INTEREST RATE

NO OF MTHS	10%	11%	12%	13%	14%	15%	16%	17%	18%	19%	20%
1	1.00833	1.00917	1.01000	1.01083	1.01167	1.01250	1.01333	1.01417	1.01500	1.01583	1.01667
2	0.50626	0.50689	0.50751	0.50814	0.50877	0.50939	0.51002	0.51065	0.51128	0.51191	0.51253
3	0.33890	0.33946	0.34002	0.34058	0.34114	0.34170	0.34226	0.34282	0.34338	0.34394	0.34451
4	0.25523	0.25576	0.25628	0.25681	0.25733	0.25786	0.25839	0.25892	0.25944	0.25997	0.26050
5	0.20503	0.20553	0.20604	0.20655	0.20705	0.20756	0.20807	0.20858	0.20909	0.20960	0.21011
6	0.17156	0.17205	0.17255	0.17304	0.17354	0.17403	0.17453	0.17503	0.17553	0.17602	0.17652
7	0.14766	0.14814	0.14863	0.14911	0.14960	0.15009	0.15058	0.15107	0.15156	0.15205	0.15254
8	0.12973	0.13021	0.13069	0.13117	0.13165	0.13213	0.13262	0.13310	0.13358	0.13407	0.13456
9	0.11579	0.11627	0.11674	0.11722	0.11769	0.11817	0.11865	0.11913	0.11961	0.12009	0.12057
10	0.10464	0.10511	0.10558	0.10605	0.10653	0.10700	0.10748	0.10796	0.10843	0.10891	0.10939
11	0.09552	0.09599	0.09645	0.09692	0.09740	0.09787	0.09834	0.09882	0.09929	0.09977	0.10025
12	0.08792	0.08838	0.08885	0.08932	0.08979	0.09026	0.09073	0.09120	0.09168	0.09216	0.09263
13	0.08148	0.08195	0.08241	0.08288	0.08335	0.08382	0.08429	0.08477	0.08524	0.08572	0.08619
14	0.07597	0.07644	0.07690	0.07737	0.07784	0.07831	0.07878	0.07925	0.07972	0.08020	0.08068
15	0.07120	0.07166	0.07212	0.07259	0.07306	0.07353	0.07400	0.07447	0.07494	0.07542	0.07590
16	0.06702	0.06748	0.06794	0.06841	0.06888	0.06935	0.06982	0.07029	0.07077	0.07124	0.07172
17	0.06333	0.06379	0.06426	0.06472	0.06519	0.06566	0.06613	0.06660	0.06708	0.06756	0.06804
18	0.06006	0.06052	0.06098	0.06145	0.06192	0.06238	0.06286	0.06333	0.06381	0.06428	0.06476
19	0.05713	0.05759	0.05805	0.05852	0.05899	0.05946	0.05993	0.06040	0.06088	0.06136	0.06184
20	0.05449	0.05495	0.05542	0.05588	0.05635	0.05682	0.05729	0.05777	0.05825	0.05873	0.05921

REPAYMENT CALCULATOR: 21-40 MONTHS

INTEREST RATE

NO OF MTHS	10%	11%	12%	13%	14%	15%	16%	17%	18%	19%	20%
21	0.05210	0.05257	0.05303	0.05350	0.05397	0.05444	0.05491	0.05539	0.05587	0.05635	0.05683
22	0.04994	0.05040	0.05086	0.05133	0.05180	0.05227	0.05275	0.05322	0.05370	0.05419	0.05467
23	0.04796	0.04842	0.04889	0.04935	0.04982	0.05030	0.05077	0.05125	0.05173	0.05221	0.05270
24	0.04614	0.04661	0.04707	0.04754	0.04801	0.04849	0.04896	0.04944	0.04992	0.05041	0.05090
25	0.04448	0.04494	0.04541	0.04588	0.04635	0.04682	0.04730	0.04778	0.04826	0.04875	0.04924
26	0.04294	0.04340	0.04387	0.04434	0.04481	0.04529	0.04577	0.04625	0.04673	0.04722	0.04771
27	0.04151	0.04198	0.04245	0.04292	0.04339	0.04387	0.04435	0.04483	0.04532	0.04580	0.04630
28	0.04019	0.04066	0.04112	0.04160	0.04207	0.04255	0.04303	0.04351	0.04400	0.04449	0.04498
29	0.03896	0.03943	0.03990	0.04037	0.04084	0.04132	0.04180	0.04229	0.04278	0.04327	0.04377
30	0.03781	0.03828	0.03875	0.03922	0.03970	0.04018	0.04066	0.04115	0.04164	0.04213	0.04263
31	0.03674	0.03720	0.03768	0.03815	0.03863	0.03911	0.03959	0.04008	0.04057	0.04107	0.04157
32	0.03573	0.03620	0.03667	0.03715	0.03763	0.03811	0.03859	0.03908	0.03958	0.04007	0.04057
33	0.03479	0.03525	0.03573	0.03620	0.03668	0.03717	0.03766	0.03815	0.03864	0.03914	0.03964
34	0.03390	0.03437	0.03484	0.03532	0.03580	0.03628	0.03677	0.03727	0.03776	0.03826	0.03877
35	0.03306	0.03353	0.03400	0.03448	0.03496	0.03545	0.03594	0.03644	0.03693	0.03744	0.03794
36	0.03227	0.03274	0.03321	0.03369	0.03418	0.03467	0.03516	0.03565	0.03615	0.03666	0.03716
37	0.03152	0.03199	0.03247	0.03295	0.03343	0.03392	0.03442	0.03491	0.03541	0.03592	0.03643
38	0.03081	0.03128	0.03176	0.03224	0.03273	0.03322	0.03371	0.03421	0.03472	0.03522	0.03573
39	0.03014	0.03061	0.03109	0.03157	0.03206	0.03255	0.03305	0.03355	0.03405	0.03456	0.03508
40	0.02950	0.02998	0.03046	0.03094	0.03143	0.03192	0.03242	0.03292	0.03343	0.03394	0.03445

REPAYMENT CALCULATOR: 41–60 MONTHS

INTEREST RATE

NO OF MTHS	10%	11%	12%	13%	14%	15%	16%	17%	18%	19%	20%
41	0.02889	0.02937	0.02985	0.03034	0.03083	0.03132	0.03182	0.03232	0.03283	0.03334	0.03386
42	0.02832	0.02879	0.02928	0.02976	0.03025	0.03075	0.03125	0.03175	0.03226	0.03278	0.03330
43	0.02777	0.02824	0.02873	0.02922	0.02971	0.03020	0.03071	0.03121	0.03172	0.03224	0.03276
44	0.02724	0.02772	0.02820	0.02869	0.02919	0.02969	0.03019	0.03070	0.03121	0.03173	0.03225
45	0.02674	0.02722	0.02771	0.02820	0.02869	0.02919	0.02970	0.03020	0.03072	0.03124	0.03176
46	0.02626	0.02674	0.02723	0.02772	0.02822	0.02872	0.02922	0.02973	0.03025	0.03077	0.03130
47	0.02580	0.02628	0.02677	0.02726	0.02776	0.02826	0.02877	0.02929	0.02980	0.03033	0.03086
48	0.02536	0.02585	0.02633	0.02683	0.02733	0.02783	0.02834	0.02886	0.02937	0.02990	0.03043
49	0.02494	0.02543	0.02591	0.02641	0.02691	0.02742	0.02793	0.02844	0.02896	0.02949	0.03002
50	0.02454	0.02502	0.02551	0.02601	0.02651	0.02702	0.02753	0.02805	0.02857	0.02910	0.02963
51	0.02415	0.02464	0.02513	0.02562	0.02613	0.02664	0.02715	0.02767	0.02819	0.02873	0.02926
52	0.02378	0.02426	0.02476	0.02525	0.02576	0.02627	0.02678	0.02731	0.02783	0.02837	0.02890
53	0.02342	0.02391	0.02440	0.02490	0.02541	0.02592	0.02643	0.02696	0.02749	0.02802	0.02856
54	0.02307	0.02356	0.02406	0.02456	0.02506	0.02558	0.02610	0.02662	0.02715	0.02769	0.02823
55	0.02274	0.02323	0.02373	0.02423	0.02474	0.02525	0.02577	0.02630	0.02683	0.02737	0.02791
56	0.02242	0.02291	0.02341	0.02391	0.02442	0.02494	0.02546	0.02599	0.02652	0.02706	0.02761
57	0.02211	0.02260	0.02310	0.02361	0.02412	0.02463	0.02516	0.02569	0.02622	0.02677	0.02731
58	0.02181	0.02231	0.02281	0.02331	0.02382	0.02434	0.02487	0.02540	0.02594	0.02648	0.02703
59	0.02153	0.02202	0.02252	0.02303	0.02354	0.02406	0.02459	0.02512	0.02566	0.02621	0.02676
60	0.02125	0.02174	0.02224	0.02275	0.02327	0.02379	0.02432	0.02485	0.02539	0.02594	0.02649

Index

accountant 92
accounting
  packages 182
  services 42
accounts
  management 90
  types of 175-176
advertising 144-145
allowances (tax)
  197-199
appointment (of
  employees) 161-
  163
asset finance 78
assets 91, 176
  acquiring 119-
  120
  current 88
  fixed 88

balance sheet 87-
  88, 91, 180-181
bank 72, 73, 77
bankruptcy 19
Basic Conditions
  of Employment
  Act 160, 163-164,
  167-168
benefits 163-165
Black Economic
  Empowerment
  55
book value 93-94
bottom line 36, 37
budget 89, 105,
  113-127
  annual 124

capital expendi-
  ture 119-122
  income 115-119
  management of
    126-127
  operational
    expenditure 119,
    122-124
  price 116-117
  revenue 117, 118,
    122
  review 124-126
  volume 116
bulk buying 188
business
  attaching value
    to 90-93
  buying an exist-
    ing 83-97
  concept 104, 105
  deciding on 31-45
  failure of 19
  financing a 70-82
  fitness for 43-45
  information 100-
    102
  manufacturing
    139-140
  marketing a 142-
    158
  model 46-57
  potential for
    growth 86
  process im-
    provements 55
  reasons for buy-
    ing 86

  reasons for
    selling 85
  risks 24-28
  service 140-141
  strategy 104, 109-
    110
  tax 198-199
  valuer 92
business plan 82,
  98-112
Business Plan
  Generator 101
buyer availability
  28

capital expendi-
  ture budget
  119-122
cash
  flow 27, 186
  flows, discounted
    95-97
  payments 174
  received 174
close corporation
  62, 63, 66-67
communication
  144, 154, 169
Companies Act 68
company 63, 67-68
competition 24,
  26, 37-40, 52-55
  price and 135
  working with
    54-55
competitive edge
  40

contract 76-77
  workers 171
cost 39, 146-147
  accumulation
    129-132
  allocation to
    product 132-133
  direct 132
  indirect 132
  of production
    110
  of sales 89
costing
  problems with
    141
  product 128-141
credit 177
  purchases 174
  sales 174
creditworthiness
  184
current assets 88
customer
  base, retaining
    145-149
  service 157-158
customers 84, 142,
  143
  attracting 143-145

debit 177, 178
debt 81
  cost of 73-75
  financing 72-77
debtors
  age analysis 126
  factoring of 80

deduction 163, 165-166
statutory 166
tax 197-199
delivery, terms of 190-191
discounted cash flows 95-97
discounts 146
distribution
  channels 155
  strategy 107
domestic expenditure 203
double-entry principle 177

earnings
  multiple 94-95
  retained 87
economy 28
employees 24, 60, 84, 159-171
  engaging 166-168
  retention of 168-169
  tax 193, 205-207
employment
  cycle, 159-160
  legislation 160-161
  termination of 169-171
Employment Equity Act 161
entry, barriers to 40-42
environment 27, 55-56
equity 81, 176
  financing 71-72
excellence, service 148-149

executive summary 102-103
exempt income 196
expenses 176
  operating 89
experts, use of 92

factoring
  of debtors 80
  of invoices 80
family responsibility leave 165
finance 24, 26, 41, 102
  types of 78-80
finances 104
financial
  administration 172-182
  freedom 15
  information 111-112
  statements 87-90, 91
financier 100
financing
  a business 70-82
  debt 72-77
  equity 71-72
  institutions 77-78, 84
  tips about 81-82
fixed assets 88
forecasts 89

garnishee order 166
government grants 80
gross
  income 195-196
  profit 89
human resources 27

income 176
  budget 115-119
  determination 116-117
  exempt 196
  gross 195-196
  other 89
  statement 88-89, 91, 179-180
  tax 193, 194-196
  taxable 194
interest 72, 73
  area of 32-33
interview process 162
inventory 126
  nature of 186-187
  turnover 186
investment, return on 36-37
investor 100
invoices, factoring of 80

job description 162

kickbacks 14

labour 109-110
Labour
  Appeal Court 161
  Court 161
  Relations Act 160-161
lawyer 92
leadership 104, 111
leasing 79
leave
  annual 164
  family responsibility 165

maternity 165
sick 164-165
liabilities 88, 176
licences 56
loan 81
  period of 76
losses 27

management 56-57, 104, 111
  accounts 90
  of risk 23-24
manufacturing businesses 139-140
mark-up 132
market 27, 49-52, 104, 106
  competitive criteria in 39-40
  potential 38-39
  segmentation 106-107
  share 53-54
  size of 53
marketing 142-158
  strategy 107
money 61
multiple earnings 94-95

net profit 89
night work 168

Occupational Health and Safety Act 161
operating expenses 89
operational expenditure budget 119, 122-124
operations 122

order 185
overheads 110
overstocking 188
overtime 167
ownership, forms
   of 62-63

packaging 151-152
partner 24, 100
   choosing 58-68
   necessity for
     59-60
   partnership 63,
     64-66
   versus employ-
     ment 60
Pay As You Earn
   206-207
pay, severance 171
payment, terms
   of 190
payments 129
personal tax 198
place (marketing)
   154-155
price 116
   budget 116-117
   and competi-
     tion 135
prices 141
   increasing 135
pricing 153, 189
   for two or more
     products 136-
     139
product 24, 48-49,
   104, 108
   cost allocation
     to 132-133
   costing 128-141
   marketing 151
   niche 55
   quality 147-148

production 109
   costs on 110
products 128
   pricing for two
     or more 136-139
   selling price for
     133-135
profit 89, 129
promotion 153-154
proposition (mar-
   keting) 150-151

quality 147-148

raw material 109
reconciliations
   127, 178
references 162-163
registration doc-
   uments 91
remuneration,
   basic 164
   deductions
     from 165, 166
Repayment Cal-
   culator 74, 75,
   210-212
repayments 82
retained earnings
   87
retention of em-
   ployees 168-169
return
   on investment
     36-37
   transactions 174
revenue 116
   budget 117, 118,
     122
   timing of 117, 119
risk management
   22-24, 28-30, 110
risks 13, 18, 19, 22

sales, cost of 89
samples 184
secondary tax on
   companies 194
security 26, 186
segmentation
   analysis 155-157
selling
   a business,
     reasons for 85
   price 133-135
   service 48-49, 104,
     108
   businesses 140-
     141
   certificate of 171
   customer 157-
     158
   excellence 39,
     148-149
   marketing 151
services 49-52,
   128, 173
severance pay 171
shareholders 67
skills 33, 42, 61
   development
     levy 207-208
Skills Develop-
   ment Act 161
social
   impact 105
   responsibility 16
sole proprietor-
   ship 63-64
South African
   Revenue Service
   172, 193
Standard Income
   Tax on Employ-
   ees 206-207
statement, in-
   come 88-89, 91,

   179-180
statements, finan-
   cial 87-90, 91
stock 92, 173, 187-
   188
suppliers 24, 27,
   183-191
   assessing 184-185
   negotiating with
     188-191
supply strategy
   185-188

tax
   business 198-199
   calculation 195
   employees 193,
     205-207
   income 193, 194-
     196
   need for 192-193
   personal 198
   secondary, on
     companies 194
   system, South
     African 193-194
   turnover 205
   value-added 194,
     199, 200, 202
taxable income
   194
taxes 24, 27, 192-
   208
termination of
   employment
   169-171
transactions 173-
   174
   flow of 174-181
transport 27
   costs 129
trial balance 179
turnover 88-89

INDEX   215

inventory 186
tax 205

Unemployment Insurance Contributions Act 161
Insurance Fund 166

valuation 26, 28
  methods 92-93
value-added tax 79, 194, 199, 200, 202
value, book 93-94

VAT
  claiming 203
  finance 79
  receipts, input 203-204
  returns 173
  vendor 199-201
volume 116
  budget 116

volumes, increasing 135
wage bill 173
work 167, 168
workers, contract 171
working capital finance 78-79

About the author

Thabani Zulu qualified as a Chartered Accountant after completing his BCom degree and Postgraduate Diploma in Accounting at the University of Natal in Durban. He trained with KPMG, where he rose to a position of Supervisor. While at KPMG, he moved to the Training Department, where he was responsible for developing and presenting training courses to all staff within the firm. He joined Mercedes-Benz South Africa (MBSA) as a financial accountant and had the responsibility of overseeing the financial affairs of the Parts Division, reporting directly to Head Office in Pretoria. Whilst at MBSA, he was responsible for the implementation of SAP within the Parts Division. He joined Unilever SA as a management accountant, where he carried the responsibilities of providing financial information and advice to ensure that one of Unilever's categories remained viable and profitable in the marketplace.

The author joined Ngubane & Company as a director, where his responsibilities involved training and development of internal staff, training of some of the firm's clients in internal auditing and finance, as well as ensuring that the clients received a valuable external audit service from the firm. After some 15 months with Ngubane & Co., he was invited to the Provincial Treasury as a General Manager in internal audit and later promoted to Head of Internal Audit. His primary responsibilities were to give strategic direction and monitor progress of Internal Audit, and to service 14 departments and three public entities around KZN Provincial Administration in the areas of internal audit, forensic investigation, risk management and corporate governance.

Thabani now manages a Chartered Accountancy practice, Thabani Zulu and Co., which offers a wide range of services, including business advisory services. He is also a director of Safefile (Pty) Ltd, an information and document management company. He has served on a number of boards and audit committees, including those of the University of Durban-Westville, the South African Institute of Chartered Accountants in the Eastern Region, and SAFCOL.

On social responsibility

The author is passionate about uplifting society. He was a voluntary tutor for the South African Black Social Workers' Association (SABSWA) and taught underprivileged learners Accounting, Economics and Mathematics from 1991 until the programme was discontinued. He sets aside time to visit schools and offer support to the administrators and motivation to pupils.

He has funded further study for a number of disadvantaged children who aspire to succeed in life, particularly in his field of commerce. He has also given awards to recognise teachers who are willing and dedicated to making a difference in children's lives.

Thabani also visits churches and community organisations to offer support and make donations. He believes that success and prosperity, values and ethics all have to be underpinned by a solid belief system, and that investing energy and money in religion yields a return that cannot be compared to any other.